Nina Kalitina

Claude Monet

Sirrocco

Text: Nina Kalitina

Page layout: Baseline Co., Ltd.

61A-63A Vo Van Tan Street

4th Floor

District 3, Ho Chi Minh City

Vietnam

ISBN: 978-1-84484-879-9

© 2010, Confidential Concepts, Worldwide, USA

© 2010, Sirrocco, London, UK.

Printed in Indonesia

SUMMARY

1.   Pierre Auguste Renoir, *Portrait of Claude Monet*, 1875. 85 x 60.5 cm.

His life

Gustave Geffroy, the friend and biographer of Claude Monet, reproduced two portraits of the artist in his monograph. In the first, painted by an artist of no distinction, Monet is eighteen years of age. A dark-haired young man in a striped shirt, he is perched astride a chair with his arms folded across its back. His pose suggests an impulsive and lively character; his face, framed by shoulder-length hair, shows both unease in the eyes and a strong will in the line of the mouth and the chin. Geffroy begins the second part of his book with a photographic portrait of Monet at the age of eighty-two. A stocky old man with a thick white beard stands confidently, his feet set wide apart; calm and wise, Monet knows the value of things and believes only in the undying power of art. Not by chance has he chosen to pose with a palette in his hand in front of a panel from the *Water-lilies* series. Numerous

portraits of Monet have survived — self-portraits, the works of his friends (Manet and Renoir among others), photographs by Carjat and Nadar — all of them reproducing his features at various stages in his life. Many literary descriptions of Monet's physical appearance have come down to us as well, particularly after he had become well-known and much in demand by art critics and journalists.

How then does Monet appear to us? Take a photograph from the 1870s. He is no longer a young man but a mature individual with a dense black beard and moustache, only the top of his forehead hidden by closely-cut hair.

The expression of his brown eyes is decidedly lively, and his face as a whole exudes confidence and energy. This is Monet at the time of his uncompromising struggle for new aesthetic ideals. Now take his self-portrait in a beret dating from 1886,

2.   *The Towing of a Boat in Honfleur*, 1864. Memorial Art Gallery of the University of Rochester, New York.

the year that Geffroy met him on the island of Belle-Île off the south coast of Brittany. "At first glance," Geffroy recalls, "I could have taken him for a sailor, because he was dressed in a jacket, boots and hat very similar to the sort that they wear.

He would put them on as protection against the sea-breeze and the rain." A few lines later Geffroy writes: "He was a sturdy man in a sweater and beret with a tangled beard and brilliant eyes which immediately pierced into me."[1]

In 1919, when Monet was living almost as a recluse at Giverny, not far from Vernon-sur-Seine, he was visited by Fernand Léger, who saw him as "a shortish gentleman in a panama hat and elegant light-grey suit of English cut… He had a large white beard, a pink face, little eyes that were bright and cheerful but with perhaps a slight hint of mistrust…"[2]

Both the visual and the literary portraits of Monet depict him as an unstable, restless figure. He was capable of producing an impression of boldness and audacity or he could seem, especially in the latter years of his life, confident and placid. But those who remarked on Monet's calm and restraint were guided only by his external appearance. Both the friends of his youth, Bazille, Renoir, Cézanne, Manet, and the visitors to Giverny who were close to him — first and foremost Gustave Geffroy, Octave Mirbeau and Georges Clemenceau — were well aware of the attacks of tormenting dissatisfaction and nagging doubt to which he was prone. His gradually mounting annoyance and discontent with himself would frequently find an outlet in acts of unbridled and elemental fury, when Monet would destroy dozens of canvases, scraping off the paint, cutting them up into pieces, and sometimes even burning them. The art-dealer Paul Durand-Ruel, to whom Monet was bound by contract, received a whole host of letters from him requesting that the date for a showing of paintings be deferred. Monet would write that he had "not only scraped off, but simply torn up" the studies he had begun, that for his own satisfaction it was essential to make alterations, that the results he had achieved were "incommensurate with the amount of effort expended", that he was in "a bad mood" and "no good for anything".[3]

Monet was capable of showing considerable civic courage, but was occasionally guilty of faint-heartedness and inconsistency. Thus in 1872 Monet, together with the painter Eugène Boudin, visited the idol of his youth, Gustave Courbet, in prison — an event perhaps not greatly significant in itself, but given the general hounding to which the Communard Courbet was subject at that time, an act both brave and noble. With regard to the memory of Edouard Manet, Monet was only member of the circle around the former leader of the Batignolle group

to take action upon hearing, in 1889, from the American artist John Singer Sargent that Manet's masterpiece *Olympia* might be sold to the USA. It was Monet who called upon the French public to collect the money to buy the painting for the Louvre. Again, at the time of the Dreyfus affairs in the 1890s Monet sided with Dreyfus' supporters and expressed his admiration for the courage of Emile Zola. A more domestic episode testifies to the warmth of Monet's nature: after becoming a widower he remarried in the 1880s. Alice Hoschedé has five children from her first marriage. Monet received them all with open arms and invariably referred to them as "my children".

There was, however, another side to Monet. In the late 1860s, suffering acutely from poverty and lack of recognition, Monet on several occasions abandoned his first wife Camille and their young son Jean, virtually abandoning them. Giving in to fits of despair, he would rush off somewhere, anywhere, just to change his surroundings and escape from an environment in which he had suffered personal and professional failure. On one occasion he even resolved to take his own life. Similarly hard to justify is Monet's behaviour towards the other Impressionists when, following Renoir's example, he broke their "sacred union" and refused to take part in the group's fifth, sixth and eighth exhibitions. Degas was not unjustified in accusing him of thoughtless self-advertising when he learned of Monet's refusal to exhibit with the Impressionists in 1880. Finally, Monet's hostile attitude to Paul Gauguin was quite indefensible. These examples make the contradictions of Monet's character quite clear.

The reader might justifiably ask: why write about personal features in an essay on an artist, particularly when some of these show Monet in a not especially attractive light? It is, however, always dangerous to divide a single, integral personality into two halves — on the one hand, the ordinary man with all the complexities and upheavals of his individual lot; on the other, the brilliant painter who wrote his name in the history of world art. Great works of art are not created by ideal people, and if knowledge of their personality does not actually assist us in understanding their masterpieces, then at least it can explain a great deal about the circumstances in which the masterpieces were created. Monet's abrupt changes of mood, his constant dissatisfaction with himself, his spontaneous decisions, stormy emotion and cold methodicalness, his consciousness of himself as a personality moulded by the preoccupations of his age, set against his extreme individualism — taken together these features elucidate much in Monet's creative processes and attitudes towards his own work.

3. ***Mouth of the Seine River in Honfleur***, 1865. Norton Simon Museum, Pasadena, California.

Claude-Oscar Monet was born in Paris on November 14, 1840, but all his impressions as a child and adolescent were linked with Le Havre, the town to which his family moved about 1845. The surroundings in which the boy grew up were not conducive to artistic studies: Monet's father ran a grocery business and turned a deaf ear to his son's desire to become an artist. Le Havre boasted no museum collections of significance, no exhibitions, no school of art.

The gifted boy had to be content with the advice of his aunt, who painted merely for personal pleasure, and the directions of his school-teacher. The most powerful impression on the young Monet in Normandy was made by his acquaintance with the artist Eugène Boudin.

It was Boudin who discouraged Monet from spending his time on the caricatures that brought him his initial success as an artist, and urged him to turn to landscape painting. Boudin recommended that Monet observe the sea and the sky and study people, animals, buildings and trees in the light, in the air. He said: "Everything that is painted directly on the spot has a strength, a power, a sureness of touch that one doesn't find again in the studio"; and added: "If a picture is not one part which should strike one but indeed the whole".[4] These words could serve as an epigraph to Monet's work.

Monet's further development took place in Paris, and then again in Normandy, but this time in the company of artists. His formation was in many ways identical to that of other painters of his generation, and yet at the same time his development as an artist had profoundly distinctive individual features. Almost every young artist to arrive in the capital from the provinces was dazzled by the magnificence of the Louvre's collection of paintings. It was the Louvre that had subdued Jean-François Millet's desire to flee back to Normandy from the city that was so alien to him. Courbet, arriving in Paris from Franche-Comté, ostentatiously rejected the idea of being influenced by museums,

4. *The Pavé de Chailley in the Forest of Fontainebleau*, 1865. Ordrupgaarsamlingen, Charlottenlund-Copenhagen.

5. *Woman in a Green Dress* (Camille), 1866. Kunsthalle Bremen, Bremen, Germany.

but was himself strongly affected by the Louvre collection of Spanish painting. And although Manet and Degas, both born in Paris, knew the Louvre from an early age, they never tired of making studies of the Old Masters and always displayed great reverence towards the classics; indeed, during their travels abroad, their first priority was always to visit museums, not as tourists, but as attentive students eager to encounter the creations of great teachers. Monet, however, preferred current exhibitions and meetings with contemporary artists to visiting museums. A study of his letters provides convincing evidence that contact with the Old Masters excited him far less than the life around him and the beauties of Nature.

What did then particularly strike Monet during his first trip to Paris in 1859? An exhaustive reply is given by his letters from Paris to Boudin after his visit to the Salon. The young provincial passes indifferently by the historical and religious paintings of Boulanger, Gérôme, Baudry and Gigoux; the battle-scenes depicting the Crimean campaign attract him not at all; even Delacroix, represented by such works as *The Ascent to Calvary, St. Sebastian, Ovid, The Abduction of Rebecca* and other similar subject paintings, seems to him unworthy of interest. Corot on the other hand is "nice", Theodore Rousseau is "very good", Daubigny is "truly beautiful", and Troyon is "superb". Monet called on Troyon, an animal and landscape painter whose advice

Boudin had earlier found valuable. Troyon made recommendations which Monet relayed in his letters to Boudin — he should learn to draw figures, make copies in the Louvre, and should enter a reputable studio, for instance that of Thomas Couture.[5]

The Salon of 1859 included no paintings by the leading Realist Courbet, and the jury rejected Millet's *The Woodcutter and Death*. Monet saw this latter work in 1860 and estimated it as "fine", at the same time viewing several canvases by Courbet which he considered "brilliant". In this same year he discovered the seascapes of the Frenchified Dutchman Johan Barthold Jongkind and declared him to be "the only good painter of marines".[6]

Monet thus immediately identified the figures who would provide his artistic guidelines. These were the landscapists of the Barbizon school, who had pointed French landscape painting towards its own native countryside; Millet and Courbet, who had turned to depicting the work and way of life of simple people; and, finally, Boudin and Jongkind, who had brought to landscape a freshness and immediacy lacking in works by the older generation of Barbizon painters. Monet was to paint alongside several of these masters — Boudin, Jongkind, Courbet (and Whistler, too) — and by watching them at work would receive much practical instruction.

Although Monet did not regard his immediate teacher Charles Gleyre with great favour, whose studio he joined in 1862, his stay there was by no means wasted, for he acquired valuable professional skills during this time. Moreover Gleyre, although an advocate of the academic system of teaching, nonetheless allowed his pupils a certain amount of freedom and did not attempt to dampen any enthusiasm for landscape painting. Most important to Monet in Gleyre's studio, however, were his incipient friendships with Bazille, Renoir and Sisley.

We know that he had already become acquainted with Pissarro, and thus it can be said that from the earliest stage of his career Fate brought Monet together with those who were to be his colleagues and allies for many years to come.

During the early and mid-1860s these young painters were still searching for an identity and were still rather uncertain as to where their rejection of academic clichés and Salon painting would lead them; but they were fully prepared to follow boldly in the steps of those who, before their own involvement in art, had begun the struggle for new ideals. At the outset they were particularly attracted by, in Monet's words, the "naïve giant" Courbet, but by the late 1860s they were beginning to show a preference for Manet, whose pupil, Berthe Morisot, joined their circle. The complete antithesis of the noisy provincial Courbet, Manet, an elegant member of Parisian society, was

one of the central figures in the French art world during these years. He struggled consistently for the cause of an art true to life and attracted an ever-increasing number of followers from the ranks of young painters seeking novel means of expression, while provoking open hostility on the part of official critical circles and the Salon jury. The main stages of this struggle are well-known: *The Luncheon on the Grass* at the exhibition of the Salon des Refusés in 1863, *Olympia* in the 1865 Salon, and his one-man show at the time of the World Fair in 1867. By the end of the 1860s Manet was the recognized leader of the Batignolle group of artists and critics, who met in the Café Guerbois and included Degas, Fantin-Latour, Guillaumin, Duranty, Zola and Pissarro, as well as the friends from Gleyre's studio. Manet and Monet knew one another's work long before they were introduced, and although at first

6. ***Boats in Honfleur Harbour***, 1866. Private collection.

7. ***The Lunch***, 1868. Städelsches Kunstinstitut und Städtische Gallery, Frankfurt, Germany.

very guarded in his attitude to Monet's artistic experimentation, the Batignolle group's leader soon became interested in him and began to follow the development of his work very attentively. As far as Monet was concerned, he did not so much imitate Manet as imbibe the older artist's spirit of questing, gaining the impetus to release the powers latent within him. Monet's development was also influenced by his active contacts with Bazille, Renoir, Sisley and Pissarro. Discussions, arguments and, most importantly, working together served to sharpen the individual skills of each and facilitated the development of certain general principles.

During the 1860s Monet had not yet determined his personal subject-matter, but he had no wish to turn to historical, literary or exotic subjects. He made it his priority to serve the truth and to keep pace with the times, and only experienced a slight uncertainty in deciding whether the landscape or scenes with figures should be the genre central to his work.

Like most artists of his generation, Monet evinced no interest in tackling acute social problems. By the time Monet's generation began appearing on the artistic scene, the hopes inspired by the 1848 revolution had been shattered. Monet and his friends lived in the apparently unshakeable Second Empire

headed by Napoleon III and supported by a bourgeoisie thirsting for wealth and luxury. Progressively minded artists longed merely to dissociate themselves, at least spiritually and morally, from the Empire. The opposition movement, which included the social forces which would come to the fore in the Paris Commune and the ensuing Third Republic, held little interest for Monet, totally immersed as he was in questions of art. His democratic sentiments, in contrast to those of Pissarro, for example did not presuppose personal involvement in the struggles of the nation. Thus Monet's genre paintings, which played a notable role in the first stage of his career, did not, unlike those of Honoré Daumier or Gustave Courbet, touch upon any vital problems in the life of society. His figure painting was invariably confined to the representation of his intimate circle of friends and relations. Indeed, he portrayed Camille in a green striped dress and fur trimmed jacket — *Woman in a Green Dress* (1866, Kunst-halle, Bremen; W., I, 65); Camille again with her son Jean at their morning meal — *The Luncheon* (1868, Städelsches Kunstinstitut, Frankfurt on Main; W., I, 132); and the artist Bazille's sisters in the garden at Ville-d'Avray — *Women in the Garden* (1866, Musée d'Orsay, Paris; W., I, 67). Two of Monet's canvases from the 1860s in Russian museums are similar in character — *Luncheon on the Grass* (1866, Pushkin Museum of Fine Arts, Moscow; W., I, 62) and *Lady in the Garden* (1867, Hermitage, Leningrad; W., I, 68). The first shows a group of friends having a picnic, among them Camille and the artists Frederic Bazille and Albert Lambron. The second depicts Monet's cousin, Jeanne-Marguerite Lecadre, in the garden at Sainte-Adresse. These paintings might seem to imply that the essence of Monet's talent lies in praise of the intimate and the everyday, and in the ability to recognize their beauty and poetry. But Monet conveys these feelings with even greater depth, subtlety and variety when he turns to landscape. Acquaintance with his figure compositions is sufficient to show that he is not attracted by man's inner world or the complexity of human relations. He tends to accentuate the interaction between the figure and the surrounding natural world: where the scene is set in the open air, the play of patches of light on clothing, or even the clothing itself, as in the portrait of Madame Gaudibert (1868, Musée d'Orsay, Paris; W., I, 121), rather than on a person's face. Similarly, the individuality of a model's external appearance and his spiritual world do not inspire Monet; thus in his *Luncheon on the Grass*, which is not in the Pushkin Museum of Fine Arts, Moscow, Monet repeats the figure of Bazille four times. It interests him as one of the elements of the overall composition, but in itself holds little significance for him. Clearly, by the early 1870s, Monet had fully recognized this feature of his talent and figure compositions became less frequent in his work as all his powers were devoted to landscape. Nonetheless these early attempts at figure painting would benefit Monet in the future, for people appear in most of his landscapes — in fields, on roads, in gardens and in boats. True, man is by that stage not the main, nor even a secondary subject in a picture, but simply one of the indispensable elements of the changing world, without which its harmony would be disrupted. Monet almost seems to be reverting to the conception of Man and Nature reflected in Poussin's heroic landscapes; but in the great classicist's works Man and Nature were equally subject to the laws of higher Reason, whereas in Monet's they are equally subject to natural laws.

Another feature of Monet's landscapes in the 1860s and 1870s is that they are often more human than his figure paintings. This tendency can be explained not only by the fact that he was painting facets of Nature that were close and familiar to Man, but also by his perception of Nature through the eyes, as it were, of the ordinary man, revealing the world of his feelings. Each one of Monet's landscapes is a revelation, a miracle of painting; but surely every man, so long as he is not totally blind to the beauty of his environment, experiences at least once in his life that astounding sensation when in a sudden moment of illumination, he sees the familiar world he is accustomed to transfigured. So little is actually needed for this to occur — a ray of sunshine, a gust of wind, a sunset haze; and Monet, as a genuinely creative artist, experienced such sensations constantly. The subject-matter of Monet's early landscapes is typical of his work as a whole. He liked to paint water, particularly the sea-coast near Le Havre, Trouville and Honfleur, and the Seine. He was drawn to views of Paris, the motifs of the garden and the forest road; while his groups of massive trees with clearings and buildings in the foreground were a tribute to the past, a link with the Barbizon group and Courbet, in the choice of motif at least. Indeed, in terms of his painting technique, Monet had not yet been fully overcome the influence of Courbet and the Barbizon painters. He still applied his paints thickly to the canvas, clearly defining the outlines of every form, although the forms themselves were already being given a rather flattened treatment. Monet's particular interest in the reproduction of light is unmistakable, but even in this respect he did not at first go much beyond his predecessors, particularly Boudin and Jongkind. Although we encounter the use of small, individual patches of

8. *Portrait of Madame Gaudibert*, 1868. Musée d'Orsay, Paris.

9. ***At the Water's Edge, in Bennecourt***, 1868. The Art Institute of Chicago.

colour to convey the vibration of light, these tend to be exceptions to the general pattern. And yet while in some ways following a well-trodden path, Monet already displayed originality. By no means all young artists find their distinctive creative personality at an early stage. Some can spend years finding themselves as tradition holds them in thrall, inducing a continual sense of dissatisfaction, and Monet did not completely escape such feelings. On one occasion he took advice from Gustave Courbet and made certain alterations in a painting but, still not pleased with the result, abandoned it and eventually cut the canvas into pieces. If, however, Monet's painting had certain features similar to those of some of his older contemporaries, it coincided in every respect with none of them. The sense of the solidity of natural forms, present in his early landscapes and reminiscent of Rousseau or Courbet, is nevertheless more attenuated, mass being represented with less use of contrast. Compared with Jongkind's seascapes, which are not entirely free from Romantic exaggeration, Monet's marine views are simple and calm. It is apparent that the young Monet was more inclined to develop his own means of expression relying on Nature rather than to imitate the works of other painters. For Monet, as for every artist at the beginning of his career, the problem of his public, "his" viewer, was very acute. From the outset painting was his sole source of income and he had to be able to sell his works. And no matter how creatively independent an artist might be, no matter how bold his ideas, the only way for him to attract attention was to exhibit at the official Salon. The Salon des Refusés held in opposition to the official Salon in 1863 had no successor during the Second Empire, and of course no painter who was just starting out could possibly arrange a personal exhibition, as Courbet had in 1855 and 1867, and as Manet did, also in 1867. To present a one-man show at that time required great courage and was a rarity. Moreover, organizing one was only possible on the basis of a substantial number of significant works and sufficient financial means. Since Monet could boast neither in the 1860s, the official Salon was his only option.

His first attempt to exhibit at the Salon was made in 1865 when he submitted two landscapes for the jury's consideration, *The Mouth of the Seine at Honfleur* (Norton Simon Foundation, Los Angeles; W., I, 51) and *Pointe de la Hève* (Kimbell Art Museum, Fort Worth, Texas; W., I, 39). Both paintings were accepted and several of the critics, including the authoritative Paul Mantz, reacted positively towards them. This situation was repeated in 1866, although it was not the landscape, *The Road to Chailly in Fontainebleau* (W., I, 19), that attracted the attention of the critics this time, but the portrait given a genre painting treatment, *Woman in a Green Dress (Camille)*. The defenders of Realism, Thoré-Bürger and Castagnary, along with Zola, who had entered the field of art criticism shortly before, unanimously acknowledged the painting's merit. Monet could consider himself lucky. Fortune was clearly smiling upon him.

In the following year, however, he suffered a reverse — the jury admitted only one of his landscapes. Such a turn of events was familiar to many innovative young painters in the nineteenth century. At first their paintings were accepted: no particularly daring features were discerned in them and the jury was demonstrating its liberalism. Then, as the painter's creative individuality and non-traditional, fresh view of the world became apparent, the jury became more guarded and the

barriers went up. This was the fate of Rousseau, Courbet, Manet and many others, but the impulsive Monet felt his failures acutely and painfully. The fact that his misfortune was shared by his friends as well afforded small consolation. The late 1860s and early 1870s were an extremely important phase in Monet's career. It is in his works from this period that the hand of an independent, innovative master began to be felt rather than that of a bold beginner. Alas, few people were aware of his achievements, for all Monet's attempts to exhibit officially, be it at the Royal Academy in London in 1871 or at the Paris Salons of 1872 and 1873, met with failure. Many art scholars when commenting on Monet's work attach great significance to his visits in England and Holland in 1871, and his first-hand acquaintance with the works of Constable and Turner. There is no denying that English landscape painting, as represented by its two finest exponents, had largely outstripped the artistic strivings of Continental landscapists.

With a boldness not found in his contemporaries Constable addressed himself to the direct observation of natural phenomena and the study of light. The freedom and freshness of his sketches, features often preserved in the finished paintings, are astounding to this day. As for Turner, Monet himself would later speak of the distinct influence that the Englishman's canvases had on him, while at the same time invariably stressing that Turner's Romantic hyperbole and fantasy were deeply foreign to him.

Yet without denying the influence of the English school of painting on Monet, its significance should certainly not be overestimated. No less important, and perhaps indeed more important, was the very fact that he visited London, Zaandam and Amsterdam, for the English and Dutch countryside, the particular character of the light there, and the damp atmosphere typical of these maritime countries, necessarily left their impression on the receptive young artist. Working *en plein air*, he wanted to be an explorer who would be taught a new way of seeing by Nature herself, and Nature did indeed teach him. One needs to have been to England to realize how sensitively and faithfully Monet conveyed the misty atmosphere of London in his landscape *The Thames and the Houses of Parliament* (1871, National Gallery, London; W., I, 166), with the towers of Parliament and Westminster Bridge fading into the bluish-grey haze, to appreciate the picturesque effects he derived from the contrasting sharp outlines of the structures on the riverside and the hazy background, dull sky and grey water.

Returning to France, Monet felt the wealth and beauty of his own native countryside with unusual acuteness — separation almost always sharpens one's perceptions and, quite naturally, the countryside of Normandy and the Île-de-France with which his whole life was associated became not merely an object of study for him, but also of worship. It was with a kind of rapture that he immersed himself in it, giving himself up totally to the creative impulse, and the canvases he produced in this state ring out like a hymn to the Nature of his native land. The year 1874 was an important date in the history of French art, for it was then that the country's rejected artists began their struggle for recognition, for the right to mount their own exhibitions and make contact with a public whom they would seek to draw towards their ideals and principles, rather than being at the mercy of its tastes and demands. This struggle was unparalleled, for in the entire history of French art up to the appearance of the Impressionists there had actually been no group exhibitions outside the Salon. The Romantics in the 1820s and '30s, and the Realists in the mid-century, for all their shared ideological and aesthetic aims, had never formed new organizations to oppose the existing art establishment. Even the Impressionists' immediate predecessors in the sphere of landscape painting, the Barbizon school painters, although so close to one another both in their lives and in their work, never arranged joint exhibitions.

The Impressionists were pioneers breaking down established traditions, and Monet, as always, was in the forefront. To be fair, we should note that the decision to hold an independent exhibition was not a sudden one. Both on the eve of the 1848 revolution and shortly thereafter artists were considering various projects for exhibitions outside the Salon, and during the Second Empire such ideas because increasingly popular. But projects, discussions and dreams are a different matter from the realization of them.

The First Impressionist Exhibition opened on April 15, 1874, at 35 Boulevard des Capucines. Thirty participants contributed 160 works, Monet providing nine, Renoir seven, Pissarro and Sisley five each, Degas ten, and Berthe Morisot nine.[7] The artists exhibited oils, pastels and watercolours — of Monet's works, four were pastels. In the future his contributions would increase in number: for the second exhibition (1876) he provided eighteen works, for the third (1877) thirty, and for the fourth (1879) twenty-nine. He took no part in the fifth (1880) and sixth (1881) shows, but sent thirty-five pictures to the seventh in 1882, and was absent from the eighth.

The importance of any given artist's contribution lay, of course, not only in the number of works exhibited. Their artistic merits, programmatic qualities and conformity to the aesthetic principles of the new movement were vital. In these respects

Monet was invariably among the leading figures. At the group's first exhibition viewers saw *The Luncheon,* rejected by the Salon jury in 1868; *Boulevard des Capucines* (1873, W., I, 292), which now hangs in the Pushkin Museum of Fine Arts, Moscow; and the landscape painted at Le Havre in 1872, *Impression. Sunrise (Impression, soleil levant*, Musée Marmottan, Paris; W., I, 263). It was this latter painting that gave Louis Leroy, a critic from the magazine *Charivari*, occasion in his satirical review to dub the participants in the exhibition "Impressionists". Fate decided that a word thrown at the group in mockery should stick, and the artists themselves, although at first taking the name "Impressionist" as an insult, soon accepted it and grew to love it.

Monet's Le Havre landscape corresponded precisely with the essentials of the movement which would be termed "Impressionism" in the 1880s and 1890s by French critics, and eventually by the critics and art historians of all other countries too. With knowledge of the works by Monet and his friends that were to appear later in the 1870s, this fact can be asserted with certainty. Two elements are dominant in the landscape: that of water, and that of the sky.

In fact they all merge with one another, forming an elusive blue-grey mirage. The outlines of buildings, smoking chimneys and boats all fade away so that only the vessels in the foreground, represented by sweeping strokes of dark-blue paint, stand out from the morning haze. The pink and yellow tones interact with the dominant cold tones, colouring the sky towards the top of the painting, and they touch lightly on the water's surface, announcing the rising of the sun, a red disc suspended in the grey-blue haze. Only the reflections of the sun on the water, suggested by bright, reddish tints, foretell its imminent victory over the early morning twilight.

The picture *Boulevard des Capucines* is no less programmatic, this time demonstrating the Impressionist interpretation of the motif of the city. The artist is looking at the Boulevard from an elevated viewpoint, the balcony of Nadar's studio on the corner of the Boulevard des Capucines and the Rue Daunou. He even brings the figures of men on the balcony into the composition, seeming to invite the viewer to stand alongside them and admire the unfolding spectacle. The Boulevard stretches into the distance towards the Opera, pedestrians hurry along, carriages pass by, shadows move across the walls of buildings, and rays of sunlight, breaking through the storm-clouds, sparkle, colouring all in warm, golden tones… Monet gives no attention whatsoever to individual buildings, even those of note (as he did in an early cityscape showing the church of St. Germain-l'Auxerrois in Paris): the city interests

10. *La Grenouillère*, 1869. The Metropolitan Museum of Art, New York.

him as a unified, mobile organism in which every detail is linked to another. The French capital had been depicted by many artists, including, in the not too distant past, Georges Michel and Theodore Rousseau, who both painted the hill of Montmartre (although Montmartre at that time presented almost a rural scene). Just prior to and contemporaneously with Monet, Paris was painted by Jongkind and Stanislas Lepine. The former's Paris was a bustling and frequently sad city, while the latter could not suppress a rather dry, matter-of-fact approach. But Monet, both in the *Boulevard des Capucines* and in his other cityscapes, affirms the lyrical essence of contemporary urban life and vividly demonstrates the wholly unique light effects that the city provides. This path, or one close to it, would be followed in their cityscapes by Manet, Pissarro, Utrillo, Marquet and other artists of the Impressionist and Post-Impressionist movements. Both the *Boulevard des Capucines* and *Impression, Sunrise* revealed fundamental changes in Monet's manner. His style had become noticeably livelier, his brushstrokes already quite varied and mobile, and his colours had acquired transparency. By now he was representing not only objects but also the atmosphere surrounding them, and influencing both colour and the boundaries of form. Henceforth Monet was convinced that forms could not look as definite as they were painted by, say, Courbet, and that local colour was totally conditional — an object's colour is never perceived in all its purity since it is affected both by light and the air enveloping it. At first hesitantly, and then with increasing freedom and confidence, Monet developed his manner of painting to correspond with his altered artistic perception. In this sense, in the 1870s he achieved perfect balance and harmony. At the Second Impressionist Exhibition Monet displayed landscapes, for the most part of Argenteuil, and the figure composition, *La Japonaise* (1875, Museum of Fine Art, Boston; W., I, 387). If *La Japonaise,* which depicted the artist's wife, Camille, in a kimono, still tended towards Monet's "old" style, the paint being laid on thickly in broad strokes, the landscapes on the contrary continued the trend indicated by the views of Le Havre in the early 1870s, the *Boulevard des Capucines* and other works in similar vein. From 1872 onwards Monet lived mainly at Argenteuil, a small town on the Seine not far from Paris. Other artists came to visit him there, as though to underline his outstanding role in the establishment of Impressionism. Among them was Manet, who in 1874 painted such well-known pictures as *Argenteuil, Boating, On the Bank of the Seine, Claude Monet in his Studio Boat* and some other works. Edouard Manet consistently singled Monet out from the other Impressionists, and in his reminiscences Antonin Proust recalls the elder artist's words about his younger colleague: "In the entire school of the '30s there is no one who could paint landscape like that. And his water! He is the Raphael of water. He feels its every movement, all its depth, all its variations at different times of the day."[8]

The foremost theme in Monet's work of the 1870s was Argenteuil. He painted the Seine with boats and without them, reflecting the resonant blue of the sky or leaden grey under wintry clouds. He enjoyed painting the town as well, now powdered with snow, now sunny and green. In fine weather he would go for walks in the environs of Argenteuil, sometimes with his wife and son, and these strolls gave rise to canvases filled with the intoxicating joy of living. One of these *is The Poppies (A Promenade)* (1873, Musée d'Orsay, Paris; W., I, 274). Across a living carpet of meadow grass strewn with the red heads of poppies wander ladies with their children; above them stretches a broad sky with light white clouds. In Monet's interpretation Nature is kind and bright, hospitably drawing to her breast all those who come to her with an open heart and soul. In his Argenteuil period Monet shows a preference for landscapes that convey wide expanses of space with an uncluttered foreground.

This sort of composition lends paintings a panoramic quality, space being developed in breadth rather than in depth, with horizontals expressed by rivers, riverbanks, lines of houses, groups of trees, the sails of yachts turned parallel to the surface of the canvas and so on. Monet's prevailing tendency at this period may be illustrated, for example, by such works as *Barges on the Seine* (1874, private collection, Paris; W., I, 337), *Resting Boats at Petit-Gennevilliers* (California Palace of the Legion of Honour, San Francisco; W., I, 227), and *Impression Sunrise* (1872).

The dynamics of the life of Nature are captured by Monet in the Argenteuil cycle both in minor, everyday phenomena and in turning-points: the spring blossoming is followed by the time of ripening, in turn followed by the fading of autumn, and then by winter. Yet even Monet's winter does not signify death, for life still carries on — vehicles move along the roads, people are up and about, a magpie sits on a snow-covered fence, and, most important of all, the changing light and the atmosphere itself live on in his paintings, proclaiming now a thaw, now a fresh snowfall, now another cold spell.

The words of Camille Pissarro, written to Théodore Duret in 1873, can be applied to all the Argenteuil landscapes: "I consider his talent very serious, very pure; he is truthful, only he feels somehow differently; but his art is thoroughly thought through; it is based on observation and on a completely new feeling; it is poetry created by the harmony of true colours."[9]

Monet left Argenteuil occasionally to visit Paris or to stay with Ernest Hoschedé, one of the first collectors to become interested in the new school. On Hoschedé's estate of Montgeron Monet worked on decorative panels intended for his host, and two of these, sold by the bankrupt Hoschedé in 1878, are now in the Hermitage in St. Petersburg. They are *Corner of the Garden at Montgeron* and *The Pond at Montgeron* (1876-1877, W., I, 418, 420). Monet's characteristic taste for the decorative is given free rein in these works, particularly in the former. In the Argenteuil cycle Monet tended most often towards small canvases and a horizontal format; here the format is considerably larger and almost square. The entire foreground of the *Corner of the Garden* is filled by flowering shrubs, rendered by lively strokes of red, orange, yellow and green of various shades. It is this bright bouquet that sets the tone for the remainder of the colour scheme. When Monet was in Paris he could most often be found in his favourite district on the right bank near the railway station of Saint-Lazare. These were familiar haunts for Monet as he used to arrive here from Le Havre and leave from here when travelling out into the environs of Paris. What, one might wonder, could he find of interests in the halls of the station,

11. *The Bougival Bridge*, 1870. The Currier Gallery of Art, Manchester, New Hampshire.

in the cheerless platforms, the criss-cross pattern of the railway lines and the bridges suspended above them?

And yet Monet never tired of admiring the confident little steam-engines with their tall, protruding funnels, the fantastic pattern of the rails and the iron girders supporting the glass roof, and, above all, the clouds of blue-white steam and grey smoke that poured through the expanses of the station.

He covered canvas after canvas here creating the first cycle of his career, *La Gare Saint-Lazare* (1877, W., I, 438-448).

The theme of the railway was not a new one in European art.

In 1843, in one of his graphic series Monet's compatriot Honoré Daumier took a lighthearted look at the misadventures of Parisians who had taken to the railway. Then in 1844 William Turner depicted a courageous steam-engine moving steadily forward through rain and steam; and a few years later the German Adolph von Menzel depicted the railway line between Berlin and Potsdam.

So what did Monet bring to this subject, already taken up by other artists? Neither Turner's nor Menzel's work could be deemed an urban landscape, the former being something of a phantasmagorical vision, the latter a rural setting being forcibly encroached upon by new technology. Monet's stations, however, are a continuation of his urban theme, his joyous poem of the contemporary city with all the distinctive

12. *At the Entry of Trouville Harbour*, 1870. Szeépmuvészeti Mùseum, Budapest.

13. *Camille Monet at the Window*, 1873. Virginia Museum of Fine Arts, Richmond, Virginia.

signs of the time. The views of Saint-Lazare station and his landscapes of Montgeron were Monet's major contributions to the Third Impressionist Exhibition, but neither the public nor the critics took them seriously. Of one of the decorative Montgeron canvases distinguished by its marvellously rhythmic structure, *Turkeys* (W., I, 416), it was written that Monet had simply scattered white blobs with necks attached on a green background, that the painting lacked air and that as a whole it created a ridiculous impression. Thus the gulf between the artist and the public was by no means closed,

assuming that the latter gleaned its information from the periodical press. But at the same time, the Third Impressionist Exhibition was in a sense the culmination of the entire movement. For example, Renoir displayed *Dancing at the Moulin de la Galette, The Swing,* portraits of *Jeanne Samary* and *Madame Henriot,* and other significant works; and Pissarro and Sisley were represented by such highly typical paintings as *Harvesting at Montfoucault* and *Floods at Port-Marly* respectively.

The fourth exhibition was somewhat less varied, for Renoir, Sisley and Berthe Morisot were all absent. However,

14. *Beach at Argenteuil*, 1867. Oil on canvas.

the contributions from Monet and Pissarro continued to affirm the central role of the landscape in the Impressionist movement. The main attacks from the critics were provoked by Monet's *La Rue Montorgueuil, June 30, 1878* (1878, private collection, Paris; W., I, 469) and *La Rue Saint-Denis, June 30, 1878* (1878, Musée des Beaux-Arts, Rouen; W., I. 470). The review by the influential critic Albert Wolff of *Le Figaro*, while remarking on the exceptional position of Monet among the Impressionists, and even admitting a certain liking for some of his landscapes, comes to the categorical conclusion that "…he has now fallen so low that he will never be able to rise again." Wolff continues — with Pissarro in mind as well as Monet: "The speed of these artists' work indicates

how little they need to be satisfied. Monet sends thirty landscapes, all completed, one must assume, in a single day. Pissarro daubs a dozen pictures before breakfast and exhibits forty such works. These adroit gentlemen really do work remarkably quickly! Two or three haphazard strokes of the brush any old how, a signature — and a painting is finished."[10]

This was written of artists who spent enormous amounts of time and energy on the creation of landscapes, artists constantly plagued by self-doubt.

The cityscapes shown by Monet at the fourth exhibition reveal changes in his treatment of the urban theme and changes in his style as a whole. The streets of Montorgueuil and

St. Denis had been decorated for the World Fair. To produce the paintings, Monet adopted a viewpoint similar to that he had chosen for the *Boulevard des Capucines,* looking down from a balcony, only now the compositions are given no indication of the position from which the pictures were painted. The artist immediately plunges the viewer into the expanse leading into the depths of the streets, filled with flags fluttering in the breeze — the cheerful interrelationships between these hosts of flickering red, white and blue flags tend to distract one from the motif of the street as such. In the *Boulevard des Capucines* it was possible to distinguish the essential features from which the impression of the city was built up — the buildings flooded with sunlight, the trees of the boulevard, the carriages and figures of pedestrians; but now the viewer has almost no chance of spotting such details, for everything, from the roofs of the buildings to the shop-windows at pavement level, is bedecked with innumerable flags. Thus the commentators who ignore the rather long titles given to these paintings at the exhibition, replacing them with a short one, *Flags,* are not entirely unjustified. The views of the Saint-Lazare station displayed new developments in the character of Monet's painting. It is painted with powerful brushstrokes which at times "fragment" the object being depicted. Similarly, in *Flags* the comma-like strokes have become frenzied; energetic marks of the brush literally lash the surface

15. ***The Road Bridge***, Argenteuil, 1874. National Gallery of Art, Washington (DC)

of the canvas and the colours, especially the various shades of red, ring out loudly and confidently. Always preoccupied with the problems of rendering light and air, Monet had thus by the late 1870s or early 1880s achieved a heightened expressiveness of colour and a powerful and dynamic brushstroke.

In 1880, at the age of forty, Monet had come to the end of his first consistently Impressionist decade. He had behind him dozens of works that were to become classics of Impressionism, and his creative method had been defined — including the approach of painting landscapes in the open air shared by other Impressionists.

There is nothing surprising about the simple fact of his painting outdoors, for many generations of artists had

already executed drawings, watercolours and sketches in oils directly from nature. More often than not, however, these works constituted supplementary material used towards the creation of the final, completed canvas. The Impressionists, and Monet more than anyone, wanted to transform Nature herself into a workshop and to erase the distinction between the sketch, the result of direct observation, and the picture, the synthesis of the whole creative process. Thus Monet's correspondence abounds in complaints about changes in the weather. He is brought to despair by rain, winds and inconsistent light, all of which hamper his work, and yet at the same time it is Nature's very changeability that is so attractive to him. How can one convey by means of paint the grass swaying in

16. ***The Studio Boat***, Argenteuil. Rijksmuseum Kröller-Müller, Otterlo.

the wind or the ripples on the surface of water? How can one transfer onto canvas the fluffiness of newly-fallen snow or the crackling fragility of melting ice as it flows downstream? It was Monet's firm conviction that all this can be achieved by tireless observation and so, dressed in comfortable clothing suitable to the weather, the artist would go out to work every day, morning, afternoon and evening. Sometimes he was even obliged to lash his canvas to his easel and an umbrella to his own body in order to protect himself and his work from the tempestuous elements. In the 1870s Monet's aesthetic attitudes took quite definite shape. The ordinary world that surrounded man in his everyday life appeared in his canvases transformed, no longer sadly humdrum, but invariably joyous, for Nature never inspired gloomy, burdensome ideas in Monet.

This optimistic view of the world was matched by his palette which, once freed of conventional sombreness, began to glow with bright, sunny colours. The expanses re-created in his paintings were filled with light and air, which demonstrated his astonishing ability to perceive Nature as a combination of many variable elements.

The texture of his paintings became particularly diverse, created by multitudes of mobile and vibrant strokes. By this time everything about Monet proved that a vivid and original landscapist had appeared in French painting. What were the tangible results of the decade that had just closed? How was

Monet regarded by his contemporaries — not the friends and colleagues who were thrilled by his art, but the public, and the press which shaped public opinion? With rare exceptions, the critics spoke of Monet in the most disparaging terms. The situation of his family, now consisting of two children and a sick wife (Camille died in 1879 after a painful illness), was catastrophic indeed, as extracts from his letters attest.

In 1875 he wrote to Manet: "Since the day before yesterday, our position becomes worse and worse; we have not got a sou, and cannot have credit either with the butcher or the baker. Although I have not lost faith in the future, the present, as you can see, is very hard." A second letter, from 1877, is addressed to Zola: "Can you and would you do me a great favour? If I haven't paid by tomorrow night, Tuesday, the sum of 600 francs, our furniture and all I own will be sold, and we will be out on the street... I am making a last attempt and I am turning to you in the hope that you may possibly lend me 200 francs. This would be an instalment which may help me obtain a delay. I don't dare to come myself; I would be capable of seeing you without daring to tell you the real purpose of my visit."[11] It was very difficult to write such letters, but Monet turned to others besides Manet and Zola. He suffered, sought a way out, and worried about his family, but all his troubles were forgotten when he was alone, with his canvases and paints, one to one with Nature; not a trace of disillusionment or sorrow remained, and no doubt cast its shadow on the joyous essence of being. After spending several years at Vétheuil on the Seine, Monet settled down in 1883 at Giverny, henceforth his main place of residence, although he did a good deal of travelling in the 1880s. In the spring of 1883 he worked on the Normandy coast, at Le Havre and Étretat, and in December of that year he set out with Renoir for the Riviera. In 1884, after Bordighera and Menton, he returned to Étretat, where he also spent several months during the following summer. The year 1886 was memorable for trips to Holland and Brittany; from January to April 1888 he lived on the Mediterranean coast at Antibes, before moving on to London and thence back to Étretat. These journeys were undoubtedly efforts to find new sources for his work, new and inspiring motifs. Nevertheless, in all his wanderings, Monet remained resolutely faithful to the central principle of his art, trying to penetrate deep into Nature, to apprehend her secrets and convey them through vivid and direct perception. After his arrival in Bordighera and exposure to the exotic Nature of the South, he wrote to his second wife Alice: "My work is progressing, but I am experiencing difficulty; these palm-trees

are a torment to me, and apart from that it is very hard to pick a motif and get it down on the canvas — there are such thickets all around."[12] In Brittany he was moved by the region's singularity and severity, writing to Durand-Ruel: "I am doing a lot of work; this place is very beautiful, but wild, yet for all that the sea is incomparable, surrounded by fantastic crags."[13]

As a result of his daily contact with Nature Monet gained insight into her peculiarities, and he created landscapes in which concretely observed, unique features are combined with attempts at generalization. One such work is the landscape *The Rocks at Belle-Île* (1886, Pushkin Museum of Fine Arts, Moscow), in which he depicts the jagged, windswept crags of the Brittany coast, the white crests of the foaming water, and, beyond, the boundless sea, which seems almost to flow into the sky at the horizon. This is indeed Brittany, but not only Brittany — it is the sea in general, its endlessness, its eternal battle with dry land. The painting is executed in varied, sensitive strokes, strictly following the form of the object portrayed — in this case, the cliffs. Monet set himself a rather different task in a landscape painted in that same year of 1886, *The Rocks at Étretat* (Pushkin Museum of Fine Arts, Moscow). Here too, the viewer is presented with a wide expanse of sea, bounded to the left by the line of the shore which rises up into blue cliffs. How different the treatment of these cliffs is, however! The crags are removed from the foreground, and the shoreline in front them is quit without substance; all sense of the solidity of the rocks is lost.

The water has none of the mobility and weightiness which are so masterfully brought out in the other paintings. The artist's attention is concentrated on the representing the atmosphere and vibrations in the air which is itself filled with the play of golden-yellow light. The brushwork is matt and pale, with the strokes playing a dematerializing role rather than serving to create form. Alongside the landscapes of Normandy, Brittany and the Mediterranean the motif of Giverny appears in Monet's work of the 1880s, returning the artist to the landscapes of the Île-de-France so dear to his heart.

In fact he had never really parted with them, but they had become noticeably less frequent. In Russian museums there are two paintings depicting haystacks at Giverny; the Hermitage canvas is dated 1886, while that in the Pushkin Museum of Fine Arts dates from about 1889. "I am always in the fields, am often travelling, and always just passing through Paris," Monet wrote to Boudin in 1889.[14] Always in the fields... In the Hermitage painting the fields seen from a hill alternate with solid, squat houses along the roadside and trees planted at regular intervals.

17. *La Japonaise*, 1875. Museum of Fine Arts, Boston.

Although there is a haystack positioned in the foreground, it does not play the central role in the composition, for the background details, which are given considerable solidity, tend to attract the viewer's gaze. This is not true of the landscape in the Moscow collection. The lilac-red haycock standing in the shade is the pivot of the composition, and the two haycocks on its right and left still further stress its importance. The background is pushed into the distance by a row of poplars cutting across the brightly-lit part of the meadow which contrasts sharply with the shaded section. Even before this picture Monet used to introduce elements which gave regularity to his landscapes. In *The Poppies (A Promenade)* (1873), for instance, the line of dark-green trees, interrupted by a building, runs parallel to the bottom edge of the canvas. Now, however Monet was attracted by the expressiveness of strictly linear rhythms, and his treatment of form became increasingly a matter of planes. Monet's landscapes of the 1880s reflect not only new searchings, but also contradictory stylistic tendencies. Some of these arose from attempt on his part to reach a certain compromise. In March 1880 he wrote to Theodore Duret that he was "grooming" his painting in a desire to exhibit it in the Salon. He also remarked on his decision to show his works at the international exhibitions of the art-dealer Georges Petit. "I am doing this," Monet explained, "not out of any personal inclination, and I am very sorry that the press and the public would not respond seriously to our small exhibitions, far superior as they were to the official marketplace. But, well, you have to do what you have to do."[15] Still it was less the search for a compromise that pushed Monet towards changes than an inner, as yet subconscious sense of the crisis of Impressionism. During the 1880s this

18. *The Saint-Lazare Station*, 1877. Musée d'Orsay, Paris.

feeling was experienced in one way or another by all the creators of the Impressionist method; Pissarro, for example, became closer to Seurat and Signac, and turned sharply towards Divisionism, while Renoir felt a new enthusiasm for Ingres and the Renaissance masters.

Unlike them, Monet turned towards no extraneous influence, experienced no impulse from without, but rather followed the logic of his own artistic development, which drove him to a continual intensification of his own experimentation. This tendency had always been characteristic of Monet, but his perception of Nature as a unity had remained constant, always maintaining a harmonious equilibrium as he represented her particular characteristics.

In the 1890s and 1900s, however, Monet's experiments with light and colour frequently became almost an end in themselves and, as a result, his harmonious perception of Nature began to

disappear. It is indicative that during this period he was already working in isolation. Although this did not mean breaking off personal contacts with the friends of his youth, creative contact with them was lost. There were no more joint exhibitions, no exchanges of opinion, no arguments. In the 1890s Pissarro moved away from Divisionism, and this marked a broad return to his old sphere of work, although his new pictures were no mere repetition of what he had produced before. Sisley, who had always remained rather in the shade, and who, in contrast to the other Impressionists, had not experienced any great creative turmoil, fell seriously ill and died in 1899. In the mid-1880s Renoir informed his correspondents that he was once again painting in his former soft and gentle manner and although, as with Pissarro, this was by no means a complete regression, Renoir's art nonetheless regained its old verve, emotional power

19. ***The Railway at the Exit of Saint-Lazare Station***, 1877. Private collection, Japan.

and ingenuousness. It was, however, the career of Claude Monet that demonstrated with truly classic clarity not only how Impressionism arose and flourished, but also how, when it lost the lyricism at its heart, it slowly died.

One of central problems tackled by Monet at the end of the nineteenth and beginning of the twentieth century was that of serial work. The principle of work in series had been used by artists before Monet, especially in the field of graphic art, with cycles of several sheets devoted to a single event, hero, town and so on. Artists were particularly prolific with series depicting the seasons of the year, some of them relying on the language of conventional allegory, others depicting rural labour at different times of the year. Before Monet, however, no one in European art had created series devoted to a single motif such as haystacks, a row of poplars, or the facade of a cathedral. Monet's forerunners in this respect were Japanese artists, in particular Katsushika Hokusai, the creator of numerous series, including the celebrated *36 Views of Mount Fuji*. Like all painters of his time, Monet was enthusiastic about the Japanese woodcuts which literally enchanted French art lovers during the latter half of the nineteenth century.

20. *The Saint-Lazare Station, Outside*, 1877. Niedersachsisches Landesmuseum, Hanover, Germany.

His enthusiasm was at first rather superficial, as evinced, for example, in *La Japonaise,* which depicts Camille in a kimono against the background of a wall decorated with Japanese fans. This element of fancy-dress gave way to a more profound grasp of the aesthetic of Japanese art, although here too Monet did not merely follow the lead of other artists, and was swayed more by inner impulse than outside influence. Throughout Monet's series the basic subject remains unchanged but the lighting varies. Thus as the eye becomes accustomed to looking at one and the same object, it gradually loses interest in the thing itself and, like the artist, the viewer is no longer attracted by the subject as such, but rather by the changing light playing on its surfaces. Hence it is light that becomes the "hero" of each painting, dictating its own laws, colouring objects in various ways, imparting either solidity or transparency, and altering contours by either rendering the boundaries of forms uncertain, or making them perceptible only as sharp silhouettes. A few paintings of haystacks at Giverny suggested to Monet the idea of creating a whole series on this theme. He began in 1890 and by 1891 he was already able to show his *Haystacks* at Durand-Ruel's — fifteen variations with a glowing or darkening sky, bright green or ashen-grey meadow, haystacks shot with red, yellow or lilac, and the multicoloured shadows they produced.

In critical works on Monet it is frequently suggested that in all his series the artist strove only for objective recording of optical impressions. Monet did indeed set himself this task, but that did not prevent him from remaining an involved, creative artist, conveying his own emotional state to the viewer. Moreover, in his first series the lyrical impulse was still strongly in evidence.

Anatoly Lunacharsky remarked: "Claude Monet made countless pictures of a single object, for example, a haystack, painting it in the morning, at noon, in the evening, in the moonlight, in the rain and so on. One might expect these exercises — which link Monet with the Japanese — to produce something like a set of scientific colouristic statements about the celebrated haystack, but instead they prove to be miniature poems. The haystack is at times majestically proud, at times sentimentally pensive, or mournful…"[16]

It is justifiable to ask whether in *Haystacks* (W., III, 1362-1364) and his other series of the 1890s Monet was deviating from Impressionism. The answer would seem to be that he was not. He was simply paying attention primarily to the rendering of light, one of the cardinal problems of Impressionism. This was how painters and critics close to Monet understood his new works, acknowledging the talent they revealed.

When Durand-Ruel exhibited the *Rouen Cathedral* series (1892-1895, W., III, 1314-1329, 1345-1361) in 1895, the friends of Monet's youth accepted it, albeit not without certain reservations. Pissarro wrote to his son: "The *Cathedrals* are criticized by many, but praised by, among others, Degas, Renoir and me. I so wanted you to see them all together, for I find in them the magnificent unity towards which I myself so aspire."[17] Shortly before this Pissarro had informed his son that Cézanne liked the *Cathedrals*.

The idea of creating the series came to Monet in 1892 while he was staying in Rouen, where, enchanted by the cathedral, he lodged directly opposite it. From the window of his room he could see not the whole building but only the portal, and this determined the composition of the canvases in the first part of the cycle. In these the artist's field of vision is invariably limited to the portal and the patch of sky above it. It is a "close-up" composition with a part of the cathedral, transformed by the skilled hands of mason and sculptor into stone lacework, occupying the entire area of the canvas. Previously, looking from a cliff, a hill or the window of a room, he liked to impart a sense of space by leaving the foreground free.

Now the subject was approached almost to point-blank range, and yet its proximity did not help to elucidate its nature, for light reduced it next to nothing.

The other part of the cycle was produced in 1893 during a second visit to Rouen, when Monet took with him the canvases he had already executed, intending to add the finishing touches to them. He again studied the movement of light across the portal and, when he saw the effect he wanted, finished the work he had begun a year earlier; where the moment from the past did not recur, he took a fresh canvas and started again from scratch.

During this second visit Monet did not only paint the cathedral from the viewpoint he had used in 1892; he rented another apartment as well, one which enjoyed a slightly different view of the building.

From here a considerable portion of Saint-Romain's tower was visible to the left of the entrance, and also some houses situated close to the tower. On both his first and second visits Monet turned to his *Cathedrals* with an enthusiasm which bordered on frenzy. "I am worn out, I can't go on," he wrote to his wife in 1892. "And, something that I have never experienced before, I have spent a night filled with nightmarish dreams: the cathedral kept falling on me, and at times it seemed blue, at others pink, at others yellow."[18]

The following words come from a letter dated 1893: "I am painting like a madman, but no matter what you all say I am quite played out and am now good for nothing else."[19]

What is known of the creation of the *Rouen Cathedral* series and other pictures of these years makes it clear that Monet could now not only paint on the spot, but could continue work in his workshop, then return to paintings on location, and then again add finishing touches in the studio. Monet had worked in the studio previously, although to all questions put to him on this point he invariably replied that Nature was his workshop, but with the years, work in the studio became increasingly important for the artist.

It is unlikely that the canvases executed in Rouen in 1892 remained untouched in Giverny, and it is certain that after his return from the second visit to Rouen he was still bringing them to perfection.

One cannot disagree with Pissarro's judgement that the *Cathedrals series* must create its strongest impression when all twenty canvases are collected together — alas, a spectacle

21. ***Camille on her Deathbed***, 1879. Musée d'Orsay, Paris.

33.

22. **Bunch of Sunflowers**, 1880. The Metropolitan Museum of Art, New York.

23. *Peaches*, 1883. Private collection.

24. *Bordighera*, 1884. The Art Institute of Chicago.

almost unrealizable today, since the paintings are scattered among numerous museums and private collections throughout the world. Best endowed in this respect is the Musée d'Orsay in Paris which holds five paintings: the cathedral in cloudy weather, the cathedral in the morning *(Harmony in White)*, the cathedral in morning sunlight *(Harmony in Blue)*, the cathedral in full sunlight *(Harmony in Blue and Gold)*, and the cathedral without indication of the time it was painted, a

work known as *Harmony in Brown* (W., III, 1319, 1321, 1346, 1355, 1360). The gaze of the visitor to the museum passes quickly from one picture to the next, then returns and runs again across the uneven surface of the canvases, studying the changes of light. The repeated motif of the portal, painted, moreover, on vertical canvases of approximately uniform dimensions, recedes, in proportion to the length of time spent in contemplation, further and further into the background, until the viewer is wholly enthralled by the astonishing skill of the painter.

In the collection of the Pushkin Museum of Fine Arts in Moscow there are two paintings from the series, *Rouen Cathedral at Noon* and *Rouen Cathedral in the Evening*. The intense blue of the sky above, the dark-blue and violet shadows below, and between them a scattering of golden, pink and slightly lilac tones, alternating with light sprinklings of pale blue — these are the colours Monet used to reproduce the façade of the cathedral in the evening.

Darker blue and lilac tones are distinctly more evident in the second painting, where pinks are almost extinguished and gold is shot with orange and red.

While on the Riviera in 1888 Monet wrote to Rodin: "I am arming myself and doing battle with the sun… Here one ought to paint with pure gold and precious stones."[20] These words could be related to the *Rouen Cathedral* series as well, for here too, Monet was waging war with the sun, and the surfaces of the canvases really are reminiscent of a scattering of precious stones being played upon by rays of sunlight. By the time the *Cathedrals* were being created, the nervousness of Monet's brushstrokes and the intensity of his colour combinations had lessened noticeably, and he was now more concerned with shades and nuances of colour.

O. Reuterswürd has perceptively noted that one of the most remarkable features of the series lies in the variations of values: "…spots of paint, both strong and weak in terms of light, interlacing in ever-new combinations of tones, the vivid play of colours conveying almost imperceptible light effects."[21]

Critics within Monet's circle, Mirbeau and Geffroy among them, greeted the *Rouen Cathedral* series ecstatically.

The greatest impression was, however, made by the review of Georges Clemenceau, a close acquaintance of Monet's since the 1860s. Briefly abandoning questions of politics, the leader of the radicals took up his pen and published an enthusiastic article in *Justice*. Upon reading the article, Monet wrote to Clemenceau: "If one sets aside modesty and my person, then everything is said beautifully."[22]

This delight was by no means shared by all artists and critics. The opposition's opinion was most laconically expressed by the ageing Gérôme, himself crowned with all the laurels and distinctions of the official art world, when he called the *Cathedrals* and all Monet's other works of this period "rubbish". The following years saw no fundamental changes in Monet's career, though the artist continued to experiment in spite of his age. As before, the central role in his art was played

by series which he displayed to the public periodically: in 1904 showing views of the Thames at Durand-Ruel's; in 1909 the cycle of *Water-lilies* at the same venue; and in 1912 views of Venice at Bernheim-Jeune's.

Two of the London landscapes are held by Russian museums — *Waterloo Bridge* (1903, Hermitage, Leningrad), and *Seagulls* (1904, Pushkin Museum of Fine Arts, Moscow).

In both paintings Monet uses the effect of a mist hanging over the Thames transforming the bridge and buildings into ghostly visions. How far removed these new works are from the views of London painted in 1871 which opened the period of Monet's creative maturity!

But at the same time how clearly linked they are, for in the later works Monet developed and took to the limit what was already present in embryonic form in *The Thames and the Houses of Parliament*.

The canvases of the London series, like Monet's other works of these years, might well be compared with musical variations. The nineteenth century as a whole provides many vivid examples of cross-currents and mutual enrichment between different art forms and genres, and Impressionism is no exception to this tendency. If it is acceptable to speak of "pictorial" qualities and of a capacity to paint by means of sounds in relation to the *Nocturnes, The Sea* and *Moonlight* by Debussy, then musical terminology is equally applicable in characterizing Monet's paintings in the 1890s and 1900s. For his now increasing, now diminishing colour modulations attune the viewer to a particularly musical wavelength and create a sort of "melody in colour".

Perhaps the most notable of all Monet's later series are his *Water-lilies*, if only because he laboured over it for several decades right up until his death. Monet conceived the idea of the series in 1890: "I have set about truly impossible things," he wrote to Geffroy, "water with grass that sways in the depths. It is something to wonder at endlessly, but how difficult it is to convey!"[23]

At that time the artist made several sketches on the theme of *Reflections* but returned to them only at the end of the 1890s. Work on the *Water-lilies* proper took place in two stages. The first cycle includes canvases of comparatively small dimensions executed between 1898 and 1908; the second stage coincided with the later years of Monet's life, from 1916 to 1926, and includes the huge canvases presented by the artist to the French state in 1922 which now hang in the Orangerie des Tuileries in Paris.

Monet's interest in the motif of water-lilies is most revealing in terms of his mature period.

25. ***Poplars***, ***White and Yellow Effects***, 1891. The Philadelphia Museum of Art, Chester Dale Collection, Philadelphia, Pennsylvania.

26. **Poplars**, *Three Pink Trees*, Autumn 1891. The Philadelphia Museum of Art, Chester Dale Collection, Philadelphia, Pennsylvania.

27. ***Water-Lilies*, *Water Landscape*, *Clouds***, 1903. Private Collection.

The images of wild crags and expanses of sea that had previously captivated him had already disappeared from his art, and the meadows of the Île-de-France with their waving grass and the busy stretches of the Seine were also by now rarely encountered. Instead he liked to paint misty London, or Venice reflected in the waters of the lagoon. But above all he was drawn to the bright and beautiful face of his own garden at Giverny.

(The author of these lines has been fortunate enough to visit the garden which, now separated from Monet's house by a fence, even today makes a strong impression.

One can imagine how luxuriant it must have looked in Monet's time when the artist, his family and several gardeners looked after it!).

Henceforth it was in this refined and fragrant world that the aged Monet was to seek inspiration.

The leaning towards decorativeness characteristic of him in his earlier career becomes dominant in his *Water-lilies,* at least in the first cycle. In the painting *White Water-lilies* (1899), now in the collection of the Pushkin Museum of Fine Arts, the artist is almost entirely unconcerned with the problems of conveying air and gradations of light and colour, rather concentrating all his attention upon the decorative resonance between vivid grasses and white and pink water-lilies.

There is common ground between Monet's colouristic solution in the *Water-lilies* and the experiments of the Fauvists, particularly of Matisse and Marquet — yet Monet nonetheless remains an Impressionist. In contrast to the Fauvists he did not turn to the use of spots of colour; his tints remained pure, albeit modulated, for he continued to convey colours by means of abrupt, typically Impressionist brushstrokes.

Still more typically Impressionist is the later series of *Water-lilies*. And yet how lifeless and limp this Impressionism seems compared with the creations of the 1870s to 1890s.

28. **Water-Lilies**, 1903. Dayton Art Institute, Dayton, Ohio.

In the first hall of the Orangerie hang nine panels, most of them linked into compositions more than twelve metres in length and some two metres in height.

These are *Clouds* (three panels), *Morning* (three panels), *Green Reflexes* (two panels) and *Setting Sun* (one panel). Displayed in the second hall are the compositions *Two Willows* (four panels), *Morning* (four panels) and *Reflections of Trees* (two panels); the length of one of the ribbons here is seventeen metres! This mania for size scarcely conforms with the manner of the paintings' execution, and indeed, in the very conception of the later *Water-lilies* one senses more the abstract work of intellect than the desire to capture a direct perception — a feature which

had always lent an inimitable charm to Monet's works. This can easily be seen by leaving the Orangerie and visiting the nearby Musée d'Orsay.

A squat Normandy farmhouse, bright sailing-boats at Argenteuil, a vast field of red poppies, breakers at Étretat, a puffing steam-engine under the vaults of Saint-Lazare station.

Vétheuil sprinkled with snow, stern cliffs in Brittany, Dutch windmills and tulips, the flickering facade of Rouen Cathedral, and the first Giverny water-lilies — how many and how varied the motifs, what subtle gradations of emotion and what a wealth of creative invention! And everywhere the winning sincerity of self-expression and endless truth to life.

29. *Water-Lilies*, 1908. Private collection, Japan.

Not for nothing would Rodin cry out enthusiastically: "…in the countryside, by the sea, before the distant horizon, before trembling foliage, before the ceaseless whispering of the waves: 'Ah, how beautiful it all is — it is Monet'."[24]

Monet's long life made him a contemporary of all the artistic manifestations of the late nineteenth and early twentieth centuries. Many of the Post-Impressionists rated Monet highly, felt his influence, and even wanted, like Paul Signac and Louis Anquetin, to become his pupils.

Monet, however, avoided all opportunities to give recommendations or advice. Indeed, the words spoken to a journalist from *Excelsior* in 1920 reflect an attitude to the teaching of painting maintained by him over the course of his whole career: "Advise them to paint as they can and as much as they can without being afraid of poor results… If their painting does not improve of its own accord, then nothing can be done… and I could alter nothing."

He then added: "The techniques change, but art remains the same: it is the free and emotional interpretation of Nature."[25] Monet rejected the expediency of practical teaching, but at the same time his own canvases taught many lessons. They taught the Neo-Impressionist Signac, the Nabis Pierre Bonnard and Edouard Vuillard, and they taught Vincent van Gogh, who dreamed of painting figures as Monet painted landscapes. The Fauvists, appearing at the beginning of the twentieth century, also discovered new truths, acquainting themselves with the work of Monet. But for the following generations of artists Monet's painting seemed completely alien.

30. ***Water-Lilies***, 1908. Worcester Art Museum, Worcester, Massachusetts.

The Cubists and Surrealists with their distorted and arbitrary perception of reality could find no point of contact with his canvases, filled as they are with the joyous assertion of life. The line of continuity appeared to have been broken.

But crucial and formative periods in art do not pass without trace. Impressionism, as one of the most vivid manifestations of nineteenth-century Realism, undeniably belongs to this category, and the art of Monet was at the core of the whole Impressionist movement.

The question of the interpretation of Claude Monet's work by artists and critics from various countries could be the subject of an extensive study, and such a survey does not fall within our scope. We shall, however, dwell on one aspect of this problem, that is, the reception of Monet's art in Russia.

In 1875 Emile Zola, exiled from the French journals for his bold articles and novels, became, through Ivan Turgenev's mediation, a permanent correspondent of the Russian journal *The Herald of Europe*.

It was in the pages of this publication that in 1876 the name of Monet could be found among those of other artists close to Zola. The novelist remarked upon the brilliance of his brush, the simplicity and charm of his landscapes flooded with sunlight.[26]

Russian artists staying in Paris or visiting the exhibitions in Moscow and St. Petersburg at the turn of the century at which canvases by Monet were displayed invariably lingered before the French master's paintings. Even if they did not accept Impressionism in its entirety or did not approve of Monet's

31. *Water-Lilies*, 1914-1917. Marmottan Museum, Paris.

individual manner, they were nonetheless unable to remain indifferent to his work.

Some of their remarks are astonishing in their accuracy, in some cases such as only an artist could achieve.

Thus Ilya Repin, in a letter from Paris to Ivan Kramskoi dated May 1875, noted the "childlike truth of Manet and Monet"[27], finding just the right words to express the absence of premeditation, the sincerity of the artists in their communion with Nature. Russian artists who matured in the early twentieth century revealed a still greater interest in Monet's work. In his book *My Life,* Igor Grabar recalls his impressions of Monet's exhibition at the Durand-Ruel Gallery in 1904: "I felt humbled by this titan of painting, who remains for me to this day unsurpassed, one of the greatest geniuses of all time along with Gustave Courbet, Edouard Manet and Auguste Renoir."[28] It might be noted that Monet took an interest in Russian culture too, though in the sphere of literature rather than painting. His letters to Alice Hoschedé from Brittany speak of his wide reading and among his favourite authors is Leo Tolstoy. "Tolstoy is so fine," Monet writes. "Perhaps you will find longueurs, socio-philosophical questions, but it is very good, everything has been studied, carefully observed. You can fully imagine Russian life." Monet singled out in particular *Anna Karenina* and the "very naïve and very lovely fairy-tales for the people."[29]

The displaying of his pictures at art exhibitions in Russia and the acquisition of his works by the well-known Russian collectors Sergei Shchukin and Ivan Morozov made Monet's paintings, like those of the other French artists represented in their collections, a part of the artistic life of Russia. They might be accepted with equanimity or with enthusiasm, rejected punctiliously or vehemently, but in any case people looked at them, and looked at them, moreover, not as at old paintings in a museum, but as at something topical and fresh. Russian criticism was not slow to express its attitude towards the Shchukin and Morozov collections.

They were written about most frequently by Sergei Makovsky and Yakov Tugendhold, mainly on the pages of the Russian journal *Apollo.* Alexander Benois, referring to Monet in *The World of Art,* was markedly restrained, but Makovsky, on the contrary, accepted Monet's art completely, seeing in him one of the seers of contemporary painting.[30]

Of all the articles published in Russia at the beginning of the twentieth century concerning Impressionism and Monet, the most interesting are those of Tugendhold. A great connoisseur

of modern French painting, he devoted many pages of his writings to Monet, and several of his articles were subsequently included in the volumes *French Art and Its Representatives* (1911) and *Problems and References* (1915). Well acquainted with many works by "the painter of the sea and the sky", as he called Monet, Tugendhold nevertheless concentrates his attention on the pictures belonging to the Moscow collectors. In his analysis of the paintings Tugenhold demonstrates Monet's evolution from the years of his brilliant successes in conveying sunlight and general movement in Nature to his late manner, when, in the critic's opinion, "the exhausted brush of the aged artist could only repeat itself."[31]

The article devoted to Monet in Tugendhold's book *The Artistic Culture of the West* must be seen as his most complete assessment of the artist; here he defines Monet's place from a historical perspective. Tugendhold examines him as an "innovator, as a leader" and also as the "contemporary and comrade-in-arms of a whole group of artists, a spokesman for the ideas of his time."[32] Tugendhold feels that Monet's greatest merit lies in his having captured the spirit of his age, an age which "developed along the lines of positive scientific thought; the light of knowledge strove to penetrate all spheres — even as far as analysis of the rays of the sun itself. Monet... never theorized, but simply painted from nature, and painted with the spontaneous enthusiasm of a singing bird. But with his tremendous instinct, his feeling for contemporary man, he sensed the demands of his age..."[33]

"Monet's art glorifies the sun, the air, the sea, vegetation... it is imbued with the joyous chimes of colours... even now it awakens in us bright and cheerful emotions."[34] Thus Tugendhold defines the lasting value of the painting of Monet. One of the leading Russian art historians of his day, Boris Ternovets, arriving in France in 1925 and visiting Giverny, wrote afterwards to Monet "of the love for him in Russia, of the great influence he had exerted on Russian art, of the care that surrounded his works in Moscow."[35] To such heartfelt words many a Russian might set his signature — both those who work in museums and those who visit them.

The paintings by Monet exhibited in Moscow and Leningrad provide all the necessary material for both close academic study of individual works and for the investigation of general problems. The earliest painting by Monet in Russian collections was done in 1866, the latest is dated 1904 — and thus "our" Monet begins when the great artist was only just emerging and ends when his mission in art had already been accomplished.

32. *Water-Lilies*, 1915. Portland Art Museum, Portland, Oregon.

On the following page:

33. *Branch of a Lemon Tree*, 1884.

34. *White Poppy*, 1883.

Notes

1. Geffroy 1924, vol. 1, pp. 1, 2.

2. Reuterswärd, 1965, p. 142.

3. Venturi 1939, vol. 1, pp. 236, 276, 293.

4. M. Serrulaz, Les Peintres impressionnistes, Paris, 1959, p. 36.

5. Wildenstein, vol. 1, p. 419.

6. Ibid., p. 420.

7. In the literature on Impressionism there is some
   disagreement on the number of paintings shown at the
   first exhibition by Monet and his colleagues. These
   figures are based on the findings of O. Reuterswärd
   and D. Wildenstein.

8. A. Proust, Edouard Manet, Souvenirs, Paris, 1913.

9. L. R. Pissarro, L. Venturi, Camille Pissarro. Sa vie-son œuvre,
   vol. 1, Paris, 1939, p. 25.

10. O. Reuterswärd, The Impressionists before the Public and
    Critics, Stockholm, 1952, p. 100.

11. Wildenstein 1974-1979, vol. 1, pp. 430, 432.

12. Wildenstein 1974-1979, vol. 2, p. 233.

13. Ibidem, p. 277.

14. Wildenstein 1974-1979, vol. 3, p. 242.

15. Ibid., p. 438.

16. A. V. Lunacharsky, Articles on Art, Moscow, 1941, p. 405.

17. C. Pissarro, Lettres à son fils Lucien, Paris, 1950,
    pp. 381, 382.

18. Wildenstein 1974-1979, vol. 3, p. 266.

19. Ibid., p. 270.

20. Ibid., p. 227.

21. Reuterswärd 1965, p. 126.

22. Wildenstein 1974-1979, vol. 3, p. 286.

23. Ibid., p. 257.

24. Geffroy 1924, vol. 1, p. 218.

25. Geffroy 1924, vol. 2, p. 166.

26. Herald of Europe 1876, p. 902.

27. I. Kramskoi, Moscow, 1954, p. 332.

28. I. Grabar, My Life. Autobiography,
    Moscow, 1937, p. 206.

29. Wildenstein, vol. 2, p. 282, 284.

30. S. Makovski, French painters in the collection of I. A. Morozov,
    "Apollon", 1912, No 3-4, p. 6.

31. Tugendhold, French Art and Its Representatives, St.
    Petersburg, 1911, p. 42.

32. Y. Tugendhold, The Artistic Culture of the West,
    Moscow, 1928, p. 85.

33. Ibid., p. 88.

34. Ibid., p. 96.

35. B. Ternovets, Selected Articles, Moscow, 1963, p. 268.

35. *Monet standing in front of the Water-Lilies at Giverny*.
Photograph by Clementel.

His work

LUNCHEON
ON THE GRASS

1866.
Oil on canvas. 130 x 181 cm.
Signed and dated, bottom left:
Claude Monet 66.
The Pushkin Museum of Fine Arts, Moscow.
Inventory No. 3307. W., I, 62.

In 1865, in the countryside near Paris, Monet worked on *Luncheon on the Grass*, a large canvas apparently inspired by Edouard Manet's already famous picture of the same name painted in 1863. This influence is reflected both in the subject, a picknicking party, and in the huge size (465 x 640 cm), not altogether characteristic of Monet's early work.

The size must have been intended to impress the public or, at any rate, to give prominence to the painting. Interestingly, the artist chose for his plein-air work Chailly-en-Bière in the neighbourhood of Barbizon, the cradle of the illustrious mid-century school of landscape painters. The fact that the future Impressionists turned to the same localities for inspiration can be interpreted as evidence of their link with the French tradition of landscape painting. Monet was not satisfied with his finished work and, returning to Paris, he left the canvas in the custody of his landlord at Chailly as a pledge.

The following year he found the canvas badly damaged by moisture and consequently cut it into three parts. The left-hand and middle sections have survived: the former is in the Musée d'Orsay in Paris (W., I, 63a) and the latter in a private collection in Paris (W., I, 63b). Nothing is known of the right-hand section. Evidently Monet did not abandone his intention of painting this subject on a larger scale, and meanwhile he painted in 1866 a reduced version of the scene — the present canvas which is now in the Pushkin Museum in Moscow. Although the painting is often described in literature as a sketch for the original large composition not surviving in its integrity, the following evidence indicates that it is a later replica.

Monet's correspondence with his friend Frédéric Bazille records that the artist was working on the large composition mainly in the summer of 1865. The present canvas was painted a year later.

In 1963 and 1973 the Moscow painting was subjected to X-ray and spectrum analyses which demonstrated that the artist's signature and date, 1866, were contemporaneous with the rest of the painting. The radiographs also make it possible to trace the main stages in Monet's work and see that many of the figures were repainted as the artist sought to achieve a greater compositional unity. The comparison of the radiographs of the present painting with those of the sections of the larger work now in Paris, painted in 1865-1866, supports the view that the Moscow canvas was executed later and is a replica of reduced size.

The different technique of the two works further substantiates this conclusion. Whereas the Moscow picture, with a subtle blending of colour and lighting, gives the impression of a rich, harmonious whole, the Paris painting, with patches of colour and sharper contrasts of light and shade, strikes a harsher, more discordant note. Monet's closest associates appeared in the picture: his fiancée Camille Doncieux served as a model for the female figures, and his artist friends Lambron and Bazille posed for the male images (the latter appears standing at the left, in the middle and by the tree, as well as sitting under the tree). Far more important for Monet than his sitters' individual features (only four of the twelve figures in the picture face the viewer, the others are shown either in profile or with their backs to us) was the scene in its entirety.

He was interested above all in merging the figures with the landscape, in rendering air and light and their effect on colours. Monet distributed chromatic highlights in accordance with the overall design — the light-coloured table-cloth in the middle, the bright green trimming of the dress worn by a woman in the central group and the red shawl on the grass under the tree to the right. Colouristically, there is little development of space into depth in this picture as all the most intense patches of colour are arranged in the foreground, along the lower edge of the painting. Compositionally as well, the development into space is restricted by the green wall of the forest, which forms a dense background. A predilection for darker tones in the shadows is still felt in this painting, which is partly due to Monet's adherence to tradition and partly to Courbet, who offered some suggestions regarding the larger painting.

Provenance: 1874 J.-B. Faure collection, Paris; 1901 P. Durand-Ruel collection, Paris; 1912 P. Cassirer collection, Berlin; 1913 S. Shchukin collection, Moscow; 1918 First Museum of Modern Western Painting, Moscow; 1928 Museum of Modern Western Art, Moscow; after 1948 Pushkin Museum of Fine Arts, Moscow.

Exhibitions: 1900 Paris (?); 1903 Vienna (Cat. No. 44); 1955 Moscow (Cat., p. 46); 1960 Moscow (Cat., p. 27); 1974 Leningrad (Cat. No. 18); 1974-1975 Moscow (Cat. No. 9); 1974-1975 Paris, New York (Cat. No. 24).

37. *Sketch for the painting The Promenade.*
National Gallery of Art,
Washington (W., I, 61).

The nature of the advice is unknown but Monet certainly was not satisfied with his picture, perhaps in part because of the alterations he had made on Courbet's insistence. Despite his disappointment, Monet must have resumed work on the subject while staying at Chailly in 1866 and produced the reduced-size replica.

The composition of the present canvas does not fully coincide with the original version. The laughing bearded man (assumed to be Courbet) among the seated group was replaced in the Moscow picture by a young man with side-whiskers (presumably the painter Lambron), and the dark cravat of the man sitting on the extreme right was changed to a light-coloured one.

The cut of the dress worn by the woman in the centre of the left group was altered, and the deep red ribbon vanished from her corsage; she is also wearing a hat of a different style. A dog appears in the central foreground of the present picture which does not figure in the Paris section of the large painting. In the opinion of H. Adhémar, Monet may have retouched some details of the middle section because after the original canvas had been cut up, its central portion contained part of the dog's figure and the absurd-looking severed legs of the reclining man. The alterations would have been to conceal the effects of that enforced dissecting. A radiograph of the surviving left-hand section of the larger work in the Musée d'Orsay shows that originally the three figures on the left were almost identical with those in the Moscow painting. It is therefore reasonable to assume that in the Moscow canvas the artist intended to return to the original version of the composition. Monet must have

38. *Ladies in the Garden*, 1866.
Musée d'Orsay, Paris.

attached great importance to *Luncheon on the Grass* as in his studies for the painting he elaborated both the landscape itself without figures and some groups of figures set in the landscape.

Particularly noteworthy are two landscapes, both of which are called *The Road at Bas-Bréau* (Musée d'Orsay, Paris; W., I, 56, and Ordrupgaardsamlingen, Copenhagen; W., I, 57) and *a study with two figures* (National Gallery of Art, Washington; W., I, 61).

There survives also a charcoal sketch on bluish-grey paper, in which Monet set down probably his first conception of the entire composition (Mr. and Mrs. Paul Mellon collection, Washington). J. Isaacson in his monograph (1972) on Monet's *Luncheon on the Grass* mentions another, pencil sketch of the whole composition in the unpublished notebook bequeathed by the artist's son Michel Monet to the Musée Marmotton in Paris. Dating from

1865-1866 is a drawing (Richard C. Davis collection, New York) depicting Camille Doncieux in a sumptuous dress with a crinoline. The drawing is undoubtedly part of the preparatory work on *the Luncheon on the Grass*. Although there is as yet no unanimity regarding the present canvas (H. Adhémar, G. Bazin, I. Leymarie, J. Isaacson and A. Distel treat it as a sketch, while Ch. Sterling and N. Yavorskaya consider it a later replica of the larger picture), its significance is indisputable. It is a unique painting, for it preserves the general conception of one of Monet's most important early projects. In his article "Letters from the World Fair" of 1900, Alexander Benois wrote from Paris about this picture:

"We cannot even dream of St. Petersburg or Moscow purchasing such a painting as this *Déjeuner sous bois* by Claude Monet."

LADY IN THE GARDEN (SAINTE-ADRESSE)

1867.
Oil on canvas. 80 x 99 cm.
Signed, bottom left: Claude Monet.
The Hermitage, St. Petersburg.
Inventory No. 6506. W., I, 68.

The precise dating of this painting to 1867 is based on the style of the lady's dress, which fully conforms to the fashions of that year, and on Durand-Ruel's label on the back: Une dame au jardin Sainte-Adresse.

In June 1867 Monet, who was supported by his parents, was compelled to obey their demands and leave Paris and his future wife Camille Doncieux, after having feigned a break with her, and go to Sainte-Adresse, where he stayed with his aunt, Mme Lecadre. On June 25 the artist wrote to Frédéric Bazille: "Dear Bazille, for fifteen days already I have been back in the bosom of my family, blissfully happy. They are very nice to me, admiring every brushstroke I make. I am up to my eyes in work, with a score of paintings under way — wonderful seascapes, figures and gardens" (cited: D. Wildenstein, Claude Monet, vol. 1: 1840-1881, Peinture, Lausanne and Paris, 1979, pp. 423, 424, letter 33). Among the previously begun pictures that he had either brought with, or had once left behind at Sainte-Adresse and now rediscovered, was a canvas with two male figures. On this, over the original figures, the *Lady in the Garden* was painted, as demonstrated by X-ray and spectrum analyses. The scene depicted was a corner of the Lecadres' garden and the model was Jeanne-Marguerite Lecadre, the daughter of Alphonse Lecadre, an eminent physician from Le Havre.

She was married to her distant relative Paul Eugène Lecadre, who was Claude Monet's cousin. Jeanne-Marguerite was famed for her elegance and the painter showed her dressed according to the vogue of that year as ascertained from illustrations in a fashion magazine of 1867, or from Edouard Manet's picture *The World Fair of 1867*, in which one of the ladies is also wearing a loose jacket with scallop edging.

This work is notable for its carefully organized composition, which bears some resemblance to landscapes by masters of the classicist tradition.

The masses are clearly defined: the bright, blossoming tree in the middle is set against the dark tapestry-like thicket, and stretching in the foreground is the green horizontal strip of the lawn, broken rhythmically by elongated shadows and contrasting with the dazzling reds of the flowerbed.

At the same time, the painting demonstrates Monet's own style of the pre-Impressionist period, particularly in the meticulous treatment of light effects.

Provenance: P. E. Lecadre and J.-M. Lecadre collection, Sainte-Andresse; Menier collection, Sainte-Andresse (according to information provided by J.-M. Lecadre's grandson, M. Thieullent, Menier had received the painting in exchange for two Chinese vases); Lebas collection, Le Havre; 1893 P. Durand-Ruel collection, Paris; 1899 P. Shchukin collection, Moscow; 1912 S. Shchukin collection, Moscow; 1918 First Museum of Modern Western Painting, Moscow; 1928 Museum of Modern Western Art, Moscow; after 1930 Hermitage, Leningrad.

Exhibitions: 1879 Paris (Cat. No. 155); 1955 Moscow (Cat., p. 46); 1956 Leningrad (Cat., p. 41); 1960 Moscow (Cat., p. 27); 1971 Tokyo, Kyoto (Cat. No. 49); 1972 Otterlo (Cat. No. 36); 1973 Washington, New York… Detroit (Cat. No. 27); 1974 Leningrad (Cat. No. 19); 1974-1975 Moscow (Cat. No. 10); 1978 Le Havre (without catalogue); 1980 Paris (Cat. No. 14).

Above: detail from p. 55.

40. **Garden in Blossom**, ca. 1866. Musée d'Orsay, Paris.

The morning sun has not yet lit the dark trees in the background, but it has flooded the lawn with glittering colours of various hues. The deep blue of the sky over the green trees is counterbalanced by the paler reflections of this colour on the dress, and the parasol has been transformed by the stream of sunshine into a blazing white halo. The first indications of Impressionism are yet more pronounced in the treatment of form, which is cursory rather than detailed. Using light, minute touches, appropriately curved yet giving the impression of a random profusion of colour dashes, Monet modelled the crown of the tree and the flowerbed, aflame with tiny tongues of colour. The present painting is comparable with the canvas *Women in the Garden* (1866, W., I, 67), where the shapes of leaves and flowers are still distinguishable, whereas in the 1867 painting *At Saint-Germain-l'Auxerrois* (W., I, 84), and *A Cabin at Sainte-Adresse* (W., I, 94), the foliage merges into a single mass, and flowers on the flowerbed in the picture *The Terrace at Sainte-Adresse* (W., I, 95) look like shapeless spots of colour. In this early work one can already trace Monet's favourite device of showing in the background a barely perceptible figure in outline, almost completely dissolved in the shadow. The silhouette which can be discerned on the lady's right, was painted over a male figure buried under a layer of paint.

The careful spatial correlations showing the perception of the scene from a single viewpoint indicate an indubitable influence of photography, which attracted Monet's attention precisely in 1867, in connection with his work on *Quai du Louvre* (W., I, 84) and *Jardin de l'Infante* (W, I, 85).

At the Fourth Impressionist Exhibition in 1879, where a retrospective of Monet's work was shown, there was a painting listed in the catalogue as *A Garden* (No. 155), with the owner's name and the date of painting specified: "Un Jardin (1867), app. à M. Lecadre." There is no doubt that this is the present *Lady in the Garden*. Wildenstein's dating of this painting to 1868 in his comprehensive catalogue of Monet's work appears erroneous. It should also be pointed out that the year 1867 indicated in the catalogue of the Fourth Impressionist Exhibition was certainly provided by Monet himself.

Part of the same scene is shown in the study *Garden in Blossom* (W., I, 69), which is in the Musée d'Orsay in Paris.

LILACS IN THE SUN

1873.
Oil on canvas. 50 x 65 cm.
Signed and dated, bottom left: Claude Monet 73.
The Pushkin Museum of Fine Arts, Moscow.
Inventory No. 3311 W., I, 204.

In 1899 the Moscow collector Sergei Shchukin bought Monet's painting Lilacs in the Sun from Paul Durand-Ruel in Paris. It was the first Monet to find its way to Russia. Two female figures are discernible under the blossoming shrub of pinkish lilac bathed in the bright summer sun. These figures, however, are not the pivot of the picture — much more so are the fleeting reflections of light on the grass, on the women's dresses, on the unfurled parasol and on the shrubs in blossom.

The handling is free and sweeping, the brushwork based on variously shaped dabs of thin paint, with almost no impasto. Some parts of the foreground are in shadow, but even these darker spots are pervaded with light and contain no blacks — the colours there are just deeper, while in the sun they appear more faded. The Impressionist principle of brightening colours in sunlight, an essential feature of the artist's later work, is already in evidence here. Monet makes very little use of glazing, employing mostly one layer of opaque paint. The picture is basically a study of light and colour, and in this respect it may be regarded as programmatic for it outlines the direction of Monet's future work. The Musée d'Orsay has a version very close to the present canvas, of the same date and size, known as *Lilacs in Dull Weather* (W., I, 203) and believed to have been produced at Argenteuil, where the present canvas, *Lilacs in the Sun*, may well have been painted.

In spite of the date, 73, provided by the artist himself, Wildenstein believes that the Moscow picture was painted in the spring of 1872. There exists an earlier version called *The Garden* (W., I, 202), executed in 1872.

This repeated use of the same motif foreshadows the artist's series of paintings devoted to one subject.

Provenance: 1873 bought from C. Monet by P. Durand-Ruel; about 1877, sold by P. Durand-Ruel; 1891 Galerie P. Durand-Ruel, Paris; 1899 S. Shchukin collection, Moscow; 1918 First Museum of Modern Western Painting, Moscow; 1928 Museum of Modern Western Art, Moscow; after 1948 Pushkin Museum of Fine Arts, Moscow.

Exhibitions: 1874 Paris; 1939 Moscow (Cat., p. 47); 1955 Moscow (Cat., p. 47); 1960 Moscow (Cat., p. 28); 1975 Moscow (Cat. No. 12).

59.

42. *Woman Reading*, 1872.

43.   *Lilacs in Dull Weather*, 1872-1873. Oil on canvas, 50 x 65.5 cm. Musée d'Orsay, Paris.

BOULEVARD DES CAPUCINES

1873.
Oil on canvas. 61 x 80 cm.
Signed and dated, bottom centre:
Claude Monet 73.
The Pushkin Museum of Fine Arts, Moscow.
Inventory No 3397. W., I, 292.

44. *Boulevard des Capucines*, William Rockhill Nelson Gallery and Atkins Museum of Fine Arts, Kansas City, Missouri, USA.

Among the numerous cityscapes produced by the Impressionists no other picture rivals Monet's *Boulevard des Capucines* in its significance for the history of nineteenth-century French landscape painting.

This picture of modest size brought on a storm of abuse when it appeared at the First Impressionist Exhibition in 1874 (O. Reuterswärd and Ch. Sterling hold that the present canvas was shown there, a view which seems well justified; J. Rewald, however, believes that another version, which is now in the William Rockhill Nelson Gallery and Atkins Museum of Fine Arts, Kansas City [W., I, 293], was displayed). The painting depicts a stretch of the boulevard seen from above. A virtually incessant stream of carriages moves up and down the road, amidst a bustling motley crowd of pedestrians. It has been suggested that the present picture shows the Boulevard des Capucines during a carnival. The entire scene is saturated with light. In the shadow the tones are particularly deep (the red and blue spots on the cloths of the passers-by).

Here Monet has abandoned a thorough modelling of detail in favour of free brushwork based on minute touches, which results in the impression that the scene is shrouded in haze. Such technique is also effective in the rendering of motion — the carriages seem to be moving, the pedestrians hurrying along, the tree branches swaying in the wind, the clouds floating in the sky, and the rays of sunshine glittering across the fronts of the buildings and sending forth streaks of reflected light.

The little dabs of colour do not model form, nor do they bring out the texture of the objects, but precisely because of this the artist has been able to convey the whole scene within one plane, the surface of the canvas, without destroying the integrity of the impression.

Like most Impressionist works, the *Boulevard des Capucines* was painted out of doors. The overall effect of this painting is to a

Provenance: 1883 J.-B. Faure collection, Paris; 1907 P. Durand-Ruel collection, Paris; I. Morozov collection, Moscow (purchased from Durand-Ruel in 1907); 1918 Second Museum of New Western Painting, Moscow; 1928 Museum of Modern Western Art, Moscow; after 1948 Pushkin Museum of Fine Arts, Moscow.

Exhibitions: 1874 Paris (Cat. No 97); 1889 Paris (Cat. No. 19); 1906 Berlin, Stuttgart (Cat No. 25); 1907 Mannheim (Cat. No. 582); 1939 Moscow (Cat., p. 47); 1955 Moscow (Cat., p. 47); 1960 Moscow (Cat., p. 28); 1974 Leningrad (Cat. No 20); 1974-1975 Moscow (Cat. No. 11).

large extent determined by its composition. Space is constructed in such a way that there is movement in every direction: in depth along the diagonal of the receding boulevard, horizontally to the left and right, and forward towards the beholder.

Continuing in all these directions beyond the borders of the canvas, the space of the landscape seems to merge eventually with the actual surroundings. At the same time the painter, by introducing two figures of men who are watching the scene below, unmistakably points out his own viewpoint. Following the men's gaze, the viewer's eyes glide over the boulevard without resting on anything definite. Like motion pictures on the screen, this landscape is best seen from a little way off so that the entire scene can be taken in. A version of this painting, probably of an earlier date (until 1972 in the collection of M. Field in New York, at present in the William Rockhill Nelson Gallery and Atkins Museum of Fine Arts, Kansas City), has a vertical format and more movement in depth as the diagonal of the boulevard is given more prominence than in the present picture where, as already discussed, there is movement in all directions, but development in depth is somewhat restricted. In this painting Monet went contrary to the traditional principles of space construction in landscapes, establishing his novel approach whereby movement in depth is gradually arrested (to become a characteristic feature of Monet's later work, particularly of his Rouen Cathedral series).

The artist had good reasons for choosing the Boulevard des Capucines as the subject for his townscape. Lying in the middle of Paris, the street was the quintessence of Parisian life. Monet succeeded in re-creating both the throbbing urban rhythm and the poetic quality of the silver-grey old city. Perhaps partly because of this, the painting continues to excite viewers to the present day.

46. *Rue Montorgueil*, June 30th 1878 Celebration, 1878. Musée d'Osay, Paris.

47. **Rue Saint-Denis**, June 30th 1878 Celebration, 1878. Musée des Beaux-Arts et de la Céramique, Rouen, France.

CORNER OF THE GARDEN AT MONTGERON

1876-1877.
Oil on canvas. 173 x 192 cm.
Signed, bottom right: C. M.
The Hermitage, St. Petersburg.
Inventory No. 9152 (pendant to inventory
No. 6562). W., I, 418.

49. ***Turkeys***, Château de Rottembourg, Montgeron, 1877.
Musée d'Orsay, Paris.

In the mid-1870s the Impressionists began to pay particular attention to decorative painting, which had suffered a decline under the exclusive control of academic artists, who would not allow any novelties in the field. The young innovators had no access to major states projects, therefore they had to seek private commissions, which was also difficult because of the universal distrust of their work. In 1877 Renoir published an article in the magazine L'Impressionniste pleading the need for a modern type of mural painting. Simultaneously Monet showed at the Third Impressionist Exhibition then taking place a large canvas designed to decorate the villa of the Impressionists' patron and friend Ernest Hoschedé, who had commissioned the artist to work at Montgeron in the autumn of 1876. One of the paintings executed there was *Turkeys* (Musée d'Orsay, Paris; W., I, 416), dated 1877 by the painter himself. Consequently, it can be asserted with confidence that two other canvases, the *Corner of the Garden at Montgeron* and its pendant, *The Pond at Montgeron*, were both painted in 1876-1877 and conceived as a single series, which also included *The Hunt* (W, I, 433). This is further confirmed by the similar dimensions of all these canvases.

It is not clear whether the *Corner of the Garden at Montgeron* appeared at the Third Impressionist Exhibition in 1877 as dimensions were not specified in its catalogue. One of the entries was a painting under the title *Corner of a Pond with Dahlias*, which George Rivière described in L'Impressionniste as the best piece by Monet shown there. Presumably he meant the present painting, yet one cannot dismiss the possibility that he was referring to the study for it, *Rose Bushes in the Garden at Montgeron* (W., I, 417). Monet tried his hand at decorative painting in the heyday of Impressionism and he set the ambitious objective, quite unusual for his time, of decorating a country house with a picture that would blend with the actual garden and be seen as a harmonious whole with it. Re-creating the fresh beauty of nature in its luxuriant efflorescence, the artist by no means resorted to illusionist techniques.

The gorgeous autumnal shrubs in blossom seem to support the frontal plane and, with the mass of trees on the right, to enclose the pond, allowing no movement in depth and thus confining the space to the surface of the canvas, a device which destroys the perspective but produces instead a riot of colour dabs. This painting, like many others of Monet's decorative works, was removed from where it was intended to belong, as in 1878 Hoschedé went bankrupt and his collection of Impressionist paintings was sold by auction at the Hotel Drouot. *The Corner of the Garden at Montgeron* may have been one of the four nameless Monets entered in the sales records and sold very cheaply.

Provenance: E. Hoschedé collection, Montgeron; 1878 J.-B. Faure collection, Paris (purchased for 50 francs in the E. Hoschedé sale at Hotel Drouot on June 5 and 6, 1878, it evidently was one of the four paintings not indicated in the sales catalogue, but listed in the auction records as lot 15); 1907 P. Durand-Ruel collection, Paris; 1907 I. Morozov collection, Moscow (purchased for 40,000 francs on May 14, 1907); 1918 Second Museum of Modern Western Painting, Moscow; after 1948 Hermitage, Leningrad.

Exhibitions: 1877 Paris (?); 1906 Paris (Cat. No. 11); 1906 Berlin, Stuttgart (Cat. No. 26); 1939 Moscow (Cat., p. 47); 1974 Leningrad (Cat. No. 21); 1974-1975 Moscow (Cat. No. 13); 1980 Paris (Cat. No. 62).

THE POND
AT MONTGERON

1876-1877.
Formerly entitled The Riverside.
Oil on canvas. 172 x 193 cm.
Signed, bottom right: Cl. M.
The Hermitage, St. Petersburg.
Inventory No. 6562 (Pendant to inventory
No. 9152). W., I, 420.

50. Sketch for the painting, *Corner of the Pond at Montgeron.*

In 1907 Ivan Morozov bought a large, rolled-up canvas from the dealer Ambroise Vollard, paying for it merely 10,000 francs, because it was badly soiled and the varnish damaged. Morozov had it restored in Paris and called it The Riverside, in accordance with Vollard's receipt. It almost coincided in size with the *Corner of the Garden at Montgeron*, part of Monet's series of decorative panels executed in 1876-1877. Either *The Pond at Montgeron* or a study for it appeared at the Third Impressionist Exhibition among the eleven Monets from the collection of Ernest Hoschedé — probably under the title *La Mare à Montgeron*. This is difficult to establish today, but the following description by G. Rivière in his review of the 1877 exhibition pertained indisputably to the composition of *The Pond at Montgeron*, whether it was the present painting from the Hermitage or a study for it, *Corner of the Pond at Montgeron* (W, I, 419): "…the side of a pond in the dark-blue waters of which huge trees are reflected". This description provided grounds for altering the title given by Vollard. The peculiarities of texture handling are explained by the decorative effect sought by Monet. This kind of brushwork with paint applied in bold broad strokes was not altogether characteristic of Monet. The painting is made up of streams of yellows, greens and blues, yet the colours do not lie in chaotic disarray. Applied in patches and staggered zigzags, they give a sensation of an undulating

mass inbued with life. Using the surface of the pond as a mirror, the artist juxtaposed the actual scene with its inverted reflexion. Owing to this symmetrical disposition, the tree trunks, which seem to extend down into the water, emphasize the picture's two-dimensional quality and give stability with their vertical lines to the quivering surface of the pond. *The Pond at Montgeron* may have appeared in the sale of Hoschedé's collection in 1878 as one of four nameless pictures by Monet, unlisted in the catalogue and sold at nominal prices. This supposition is based on the following considerations: in 1968 M. Bodelsen published in The Burlington Magazine the records of the 1878 Hoschedé sale, which she had discovered in the archives, and which listed many Monets. Recorded as items 6, 7, 15 and 16 were nameless paintings by Monet, not included in the sale catalogue. Two of them were bought by G. Petit for seventy-five and thirty-eight francs, one by J.-B. Faure for fifty francs and one by De Bellio for thirty-five francs. The present writer believes that the canvas purchased by J.-B. Faure is *The Pond at Montgeron*, now in the Hermitage. When Morozov purchased it from Vollard, the dealer had it in a roll and its varnish was soiled, thus, like the other three pictures, it had probably appeared at the Hotel Drouot rolled up. Not examined prior to the sale and not included in the catalogue, it sold for a much lower price than did Monet's other works.

Provenance: E. Hoschedé collection, Montgeron (commissioned for the Chateau de Rottembourg); 1878 A. Vollard collection, Paris; 1907 I. Morozov collection, Moscow; 1918 Second Museum of Modern Western Painting, Moscow; 1928 Museum of Modern Western Art, Moscow; after 1931 Hermitage, Leningrad.

Exhibitions: 1877 Paris (Cat. No. 91?); 1974 Leningrad (Cat. No. 22); 1974-1975 Moscow (Cat. No. 14); 1979 Kyoto, Tokyo, Kamakura (Cat. No. 8).

THE ROCKS AT BELLE-ÎLE

1886.
Oil on canvas. 65 x 81 cm.
Signed and dated, bottom right:
Claude Monet 86.
The Pushkin Museum of Fine Arts, Moscow.
Inventory No. 3310. W., II, 1084.

Marine subjects play a prominent part in Monet's œuvre. The artist's love of the sea was probably awakened when he lived in Le Havre, where he learned the rudiments of painting under Eugène Boudin. Monet painted seascapes all his life, but the best of them are those produced in the 1880s at Belle-Île and Étretat. In September and October 1886 the artist worked at picturesque Belle-Île and it was then, in all likelihood, that the present canvas was painted.

The gloom of the place invested the painting with a stern atmosphere; the colours are harsh and clashing patches of white, blue, green and brownish-violet, applied in energetic, almost impasted strokes of varying sizes and shapes. This dynamic handling evokes a sense of restless motion, the elements ever at work and the sea never the same. The mercurial sea is the keynote of the painting, everything else — the artist's usual interest in the intricate play of reflected sunshine, the effects of light on colours, etc. — being less significant. Monet was completely captivated by the stern romance of the sea and rocks.

This spot was painted by Monet time and again, therefore versions of the motif are to be found in many collections in different parts of the world. The same year, 1886, Monet portrayed the sea at Belle-Île in three other pictures, two of which are in the Musée d'Orsay in Paris (W., II, 1100, 1116) and one in a private collection in Copenhagen (W., II, 1086). Besides the Copenhagen painting, close to the present marine are canvases depicting rocks at Belle-Île (W., II, 1085, 1087-1089). D. Wildenstein calls the Moscow painting *Pyramids of Porte-Coton. Stormy Sea.*

Provenance: 1887 G. Petit collection, Paris: 1889 P. Aubry collection, Paris; 1897 P. Durand-Ruel collection, Paris; 1898 S. Shchukin collection, Moscow; 1918 First Museum of Modern Western Painting, Moscow; 1928 Museum of Modern Western Art, Moscow; after 1948 Pushkin Museum of Fine Arts, Moscow.

Exhibitions: 1939 Moscow (Cat., p. 47); 1955 Moscow (Cat., p. 47); 1960 Moscow (Cat., p. 28); 1974-1975 Moscow (Cat. No. 15).

53. *The Rocks at Belle-Île*, photograph.

54. *The Rocks at Belle-Île*, 1886. Musée d'Orsay, Paris.

55. *The Rock Needle of Porte-Coton*. Sale, Sotheby's, London, November 29, 1972.

56.

THE ROCKS
AT ÉTRETAT

1886.
Oil on canvas. 66 x 81 cm.
Signed and dated, bottom left:
Claude Monet 86.
The Pushkin Museum of Fine Arts, Moscow.
Inventory No. 3308 W., II, 1046.

Like many artists of his day and earlier times, Monet repeatedly sojourned and worked on the coast of Normandy, where Delacroix and Courbet had once painted many marine scenes. Between 1883 and 1886 Monet often visited Étretat and some of his seascapes were produced at that time. Their recurrent motif is a cliff jutting out far into the sea, as in the present picture, which was done from the d'Amont rock near the Payen house. On November 19, 1885, Monet wrote to A. Hoschedé: "…at last I've done the departure of boats near the Payen house" (W., II, 629).

The colour range of this painting is entirely different from the palette Monet employed in the seascape painted at Belle-Île. A golden-yellow tonality predominates in the present view of Étretat, while the bluish and greenish boats add colour accents, bringing out more clearly spatial correlations. Earlier views of Étretat are known; for example, the Musée

d'Orsay has his *Stormy Sea at Étretat*, which is generally assigned to 1868-1869 (W., I, 127). The same museum possesses another view of the place painted by Monet a decade later, in 1883 (W., II, 828).

There survives a letter from Monet to Durand-Ruel written at Giverny on September 16, 1885, intimating that the singer J.-B. Faure had invited the artist to come and stay with him at Étretat. It is likely that Monet accepted such invitations more than once, and that this landscape was produced on one of his visits to Étretat.

Closest to the present marine is the painting *Fishing Boats Leaving the Port* (W., II, 1047) painted from the same spot but at a different time of the day and under different weather conditions. Wildenstein calls the Moscow painting *Fishing Boats Leaving Étretat*. There is a drawing for it in the Musée Marmottan (No. 5131, f° 26 verso).

Provenance: 1877 Boussod, Valadon et Cie, collection, Paris; 1889 Bugle collection, Paris; 1891 P. Durand-Ruel collection, Paris; 1893 Guy de Chollet collection, Paris; 1893 P. Durand-Ruel collection, Paris; 1898 S. Shchukin collection, Moscow; 1918 First Museum of Modern Western Painting, Moscow; 1928 Museum of Modern Western Art, Moscow; after 1948 Pushkin Museum of Fine Arts, Moscow.

Exhibitions: 1939 Moscow (Cat., p. 47); 1955 Moscow (Cat., p. 47); 1960 Moscow (Cat., p. 28); 1966-1967 Tokyo, Kyoto (Cat. No. 51); 1972 Otterlo (Cat. No. 38); 1974-1975 Moscow (Cat. No.1 6).

57. *Étretat, Sunset*, 1883.

58. *Étretat, The Rain*, 1885-1886.

59. **The Rock Needle through the Porte d'Aval**, 1885-1886.

HAYSTACK AT GIVERNY

1886.
Formerly entitled A Haystack.
Oil on canvas. 61 x 81 cm.
Signed and dated, bottom right:
Claude Monet. 86.
The Hermitage, St. Petersburg.
Inventory No. 6563. W., II. 1073.

Monet's later period is associated with the village of Giverny, where he settled in 1883. At this stage, instead of the free, spontaneous manner of his earlier works, Monet employed a more analytical approach, scrutinizing his subjects in series of paintings. The effects of atmosphere and light now served as points of departure in search of colouristic harmonies of infinite diversity, reminiscent of subtle musical variations.

In the transitional period of the 1880s two trends appeared in Monet's landscapes: on the one hand he was interested in dramatic views of nature with the elements at work; on the other he was attracted by the serenity of the quiet countryside, where he had returned after long travels in the south and north of France. The fields and meadows of Giverny appeared on his canvases, now and then enlivened by a cluster of cottages, as in the present picture, executed in the summer of 1886 soon after the artist's return from Holland, where he painted *The Tulip Field in Holland* (W., II, 1067). The peaceful contemplative atmosphere, so characteristic of most works produced at Giverny, is achieved here by means of the composition based on contrasting colour zones alternating in parallel rows along the horizontal format. Quite in tune with this unhurried rhythm of horizontal lines are the village cottages which, playing a fairly significant role in the overall design, make the title *A Haystack* inappropriate. A few years later the artist was to paint a large series of *Haystacks*, but here the stack is not yet dominant in the pictorial space, no riot of colour surrounds it as in that later series. Although even in this painting the day does emanate multitudes of luminous hues, its primary tonality is close to that of the yellow strip of grass, and the stack blends indistinguishably with the bright red-green surface of the field, its peak gently interrupting the horizontal lines. Transitional features remanifest also in the construction of space. The middle ground, with the rustic houses visible through the thick verdure, is represented with considerable clarity of form, whereas the foreground, worked with light opaque layers of paint, has already lost structural coherence of objects, its hues merely hinting at the things represented — yellow grain, green grass and red flowers.

Provenance: 1905 S. Shchukin collection, Moscow; 1918 First Museum of Modern Western Painting, Moscow; 1928 Museum of Modern Western Art, Moscow; after 1930 Hermitage, Leningrad.

Exhibitions: 1955 Moscow (Cat., p. 47); 1956 Leningrad (Cat., p. 41); 1960 Moscow (Cat., p. 28); 1972 Otterlo (Cat. No. 37); 1974 Leningrad (Cat. No. 23); 1974-1975 Moscow (Cat. No. 18); 1981 Mexico (Cat. No. 23).

61.

MEADOWS
AT GIVERNY

1888.
Oil on canvas. 92 x 80 cm.
Signed and dated, bottom left:
Claude Monet 88.
The Hermitage, St. Petersburg.
Inventory No. 7721. W., III, 1202.

The painting *Meadows at Giverny* is one of a group of works produced in the summer months of 1887 and 1888. Closely related compositionally and differing only in minor details, they nevertheless do not constitute a series and are generally regarded as independent works (*Walk in Dull Weather*, W., III, 1203; *Landscape with Figures, Giverny,* Art Institute of Chicago, USA, W., III, 1204).

The Hermitage version differs from its counterparts in its extreme concision of pictorial design. The simplicity of the composition accents the incessant vibration of the air and the play of light, owing to which the vacant and unconfirmed space of the meadow does not strike the viewer as empty. The light, fragmented dabs of contrasting tones seem to flutter over the canvas, creating the impression of a soft glow. As in most of the artist's later works, the sky is the primary chromatic element of the landscape. Its opaline hues highlight the shimmering colours of the meadow and set off the outlines of the poplars, which are traced out in green and blue after the fashion of exquisite lacework. The whole scene is infused with an atmosphere of contemplation and peace, and the artist's palette has reached a fully maturity of expression.

Provenance: 1889 P. Durand-Ruel collection (purchased from C. Monet in June 1889), Paris; 1892 D. Cochin collection, Paris; 1897 P. Durand-Ruel collection, Paris; 1899 S. Shchukin collection, Moscow; 1918 First Museum of Modern Western Painting, Moscow; 1928 Museum of Modern Western Art, Moscow; after 1934 Hermitage, Leningrad.

Exhibitions: 1956 Leningrad (Cat., p. 41); 1960 Moscow (Cat., p. 28); 1974 Leningrad (Cat. No. 25); 1978 Le Havre (without catalogue).

62. *Landscape with Figures, Giverny*. Private collection, USA.

63. *The Promenade, the Woman with a Parasol*. National Gallery of Art, Washington D.C..

64. *The Branch of the Seine at Giverny, Fog*, 1897. North Carolina Museum of Art, Raleigh, North Carolina.

Page 85 :

65. *Morning on the Seine*, 1897. Private collection, USA.

66. *Branch of the Seine at Giverny, Daybreak*, 1897. Hiroshima Museum of Art, Hiroshima.

THE POPPY FIELD

About 1887.
Oil on canvas. 59 x 60 cm.
Signed, bottom right: Claude Monet.
The Hermitage, St. Petersburg.
Inventory No 9004. W., III. 1255.

The poppy field theme never lost its attraction for the artist. Before going to Holland in 1886 and elaborating the red tones of *The Tulip Field* (W., II, 1067), Monet treated this theme in a way peculiarly his own. More often than not he depicted the golden-green expanse of field with the scarlet flashes of poppies running through it. This is exemplified by *The Poppies (A Promenade)* of 1873 (W., I, 274) and *The Poppy Field at Lavacourt* of 1881 (W., I, 677). In pictures on the poppy field motif done after 1886, the artist no longer cares about revealing the actual shapes of the flowers, but dissolves them into a continuous stream of red tones interspersed with greens.

It is precisely in this manner that the Hermitage canvas is executed. Its dating presents great difficulty. Wildenstein assigns the picture to 1890, linking it with a series of four landscapes devoted to one and the same motif (W., III, 1251, 1252, 1253, and 1254, of which two are dated 1890 and 1891 by the artist himself). However, the Hermitage canvas differs from the landscape series in both theme and execution. While in all the landscapes of this series Monet repeatedly depicts the slope of a hill in the right-hand part of the composition, just behind the trees, in the present canvas he unfolds the chain of hills along the entire horizontal of the picture far away from the poplars. A forest massif visible in front of the hills is absent in the landscape series. By its painterly features the Hermitage canvas shares greater affinity with *Lucerne and Poppies*, dated 1887 by the artist (W., III, 1146) and showing a locality south of Giverny.

This landscape echoes the Hermitage painting above all in the rendering of the sky covered by small white-edged clouds. The thick, multi-layered texture of brushstrokes typical of the Hermitage canvas can also be seen in other works by Monet dating from 1887, such as *Barque* (W., III, 1154) and *Barques at Giverny* (W., III, 1151). Consequently, there is some reason to believe that the Hermitage picture was painted in 1887, when the artist worked on *Lucerne and Poppies*.

Provenance: G. Feydeau collection, Paris; 1901 Bernheim-Jeune Gallery, Paris (purchased in the G. Feydeau sale at the Hotel Drouot, February 11, 1901, lot 74); 1903 M. Morozova collection, Moscow; 1910 Tretyakov Gallery, Moscow (gift of M. Morozova); 1925 Second Museum of Modern Western Painting, Moscow; 1928 Museum of Modern Western Art, Moscow; after 1948 Hermitage, Leningrad.

Exhibitions: 1889 Paris (without catalogue); 1939 Moscow (Cat., p. 19); 1955 Moscow (Cat., p. 47); 1956 Leningrad (Cat., p. 41); 1965-1966 Bordeaux, Paris (Cat. No. 67); 1966-1967 Tokyo, Kyoto (Cat. No. 50); 1974 Leningrad (Cat. No. 24); 1974-1975 Moscow (Cat. No. 18).

68. *The Poppy Field, near Giverny*, 1885.

69. *The Poppy Field near Vétheuil*, 1879.

70. *The Poppy Field*, 1890.

71. *Poppies at Argenteuil*, 1873.

72. *Sketch for a Figure in Open Air* (to the left). Musée d'Orsay, Paris.

73. **Sketch for a Figure in Open Air** (to the right). Musée d'Orsay, Paris.

HAYSTACK
NEAR GIVERNY

1889,
Oil on canvas. 64.5 x 81 cm.
Signed, bottom left:
Claude Monet.
The Pushkin Museum of Fine Arts, Moscow.
Inventory No. 3898. W., II, 900.

From 1883 onwards Monet often worked at Giverny, repeatedly painting the motif of haystacks. The earliest canvases in the series were probably executed there in the mid 1880s. Wildenstein dates the present painting to 1884. Many well-known pictures in this series are now in the USA, in private collections or museums (W., III, 1268; W., III, 1270, etc). The present canvas is undated but it is known to have been exhibited at Durand-Ruel's in March 1907 as one of seventeen works by Monet from the J.-B. Faure collection and catalogued as painted in 1889. Some researchers, however, date the Moscow picture differently: M. Orlova believes that the entire haystack series originated in 1891, whereas D. Pataky assigns the present painting to 1899. The date suggested by Wildenstein seems to be more accurate, as the painting in a private collection in the USA (W., II, 901), which repeats the motif of the present canvas, is dated 1884. The same motif is used in another painting in a private collection in the USA (W., II, 902).

It seems that the Moscow painting could have been executed in 1884-1889. The picture is notable for its extraordinary freshness and purity of colour. The dominant tones are the deep blues and greens of the poplars' foliage. Unlike some of Monet's works of the 1870s (e.g. Lilacs in the Sun) the colours in this picture have not faded or bleached in sunlight. Such intensity of colour is characteristic of many of the works by Monet painted in the 1880s.

At the same time, the artist remained faithful to the principles of Impressionism even in this painting. His main objective was a sense of immediacy, the rendering of lighting at a certain time of day.

A letter from Paul Durand-Ruel to Ivan Morozov has survived in the archives of the Pushkin Museum of Fine Arts. The French collector wrote it on May 27, 1907, to acknowledge the receipt of 50,000 francs for two paintings by Monet, one of which was the present picture, *Haystack near Giverny.*

Provenance: 1906 J.-B. Faure collection, Paris; 1907 P. Durand-Ruel collection, Paris (until 14 July); 1907 I. Morozov collection, Moscow (after 14 July); 1918 Second Museum of Modern Western Painting, Moscow; 1928 Museum of Modern Western Art, Moscow; after 1948 Pushkin Museum of Fine Arts, Moscow.

Exhibitions: 1906 Paris (Cat. No. 17); 1939 Moscow (Cat. p. 48); 1955 Moscow (Cat., p. 48); 1960 Moscow (Cat. p. 29); 1972 Otterlo (Cat. No. 39); 1972 Prague (Cat. No. 26); 1974-1975 Moscow (Cat. No. 19).

75. *Haystacks at Giverny in Muted Sunlight*, 1888-1889.

76. *Haystacks, End of an Autumn Day*, 1891.

ROUEN CATHEDRAL
IN THE EVENING

1894.
Oil on canvas. 100 x 65 cm.
Signed and dated, bottom left:
Claude Monet 94.
The Pushkin Museum of Fine Arts, Moscow.
Inventory No. 3312. W., III 1326.

78. *Under the Poplars, Sunlight Effect*, 1887.
Staatsgalerie, Stuttgart, Germany.

Monet liked to use one and the same motif repeatedly. Thus between 1892 and 1895 he produced the famous series of twenty paintings devoted to Rouen Cathedral. The most remarkable works in that series date from 1894, as do the two paintings reproduced in this volume. Monet arrived at Rouen in February 1892 and boarded in a house opposite Rouen Cathedral. From this viewpoint, at close range, the main paintings in the Cathedral series were executed. It determined the design of all the pictures in the series: the facade of the cathedral occupies almost the entire canvas, the soaring towers cut off by the top edge of the picture.

The upper part of the facade is painted in golden and pinkish hues, and its shadowed lower part in lilac-pink dabs. The summer sky shows above as a patch of blue. The stone arches over the portals are almost ethereal and recognizable only from their paler shadows; the pattern of the rose window dissolves in the dark bluish shade; the outlines of other elements of the building have lost all distinctness; indeed everything looks like one vibrant, palpitating mass of colour. The cathedral is flooded with warm evening light. The sun has already begun to sink and its rays, falling on the vertical surface almost at a right angle, make the cold stone scintillate. The houses on the other side of the square cast long shadows extending as far as the lower part of the cathedral façade. In his desire to capture all the wealth and variety of lighting effects on the cathedral's surface the artist passed quickly from one canvas to another as the lighting changed with the movement of the sun. The Cathedral series can be regarded as the culmination of the Impressionist method in Monet's work. The entire set was first displayed in the year of its completion, 1895; later it was often exhibited both in France and abroad. At present the canvases making up the Rouen Cathedral series are in different museums of the world, the Musée d'Orsay in Paris boasting five of them (W., III, 1319, 1321, 1346, 1355, 1360).

Provenance: 1898 P. Durand-Ruel collection, Paris; 1901 S. Shchukin collection, Moscow; 1918 First Museum of Modern Western Painting, Moscow; 1928 Museum of Modern Western Art, Moscow; after 1948 Pushkin Museum of Fine Arts, Moscow.

Exhibitions: 1895 Paris; 1955 Moscow (Cat., p. 47); 1960 Moscow (Cat., p. 28); 1974 Leningrad (Cat. No. 26); 1974-1975 Moscow (Cat. No. 20).

Page 100 :

79. **Rouen Cathedral, Grey and Pink Symphony**, 1892. National Museum of Wales, Cardiff, England.

Page 101 :

80. **The Portal, Morning Fog**, 1893. Museum Folkwang, Essen, Germany.

Page 102 :

81. **Rouen Cathedral, Portal of Saint-Romain's Tower (Full Sun)**, 1894. Musée d'Orsay, Paris.

82.

ROUEN CATHEDRAL
AT NOON

1894.
Oil on canvas. 101 x 65 cm.
Signed and dated, bottom left:
Claude Monet 94.
The Pushkin Museum of Fine Arts, Moscow.
Inventory No. 3313. W., III, 1350.

This picture shows the central section of the cathedral front surmounted by a tower, the upper part lit by slanting rays of sunshine and the lower steeped in shadow. The façade of the cathedral fills almost the whole canvas, giving the impression that the artist painted it standing nearby. Yet no details of the building's Gothic massiveness or its structural parts are discernible, nor can one feel the texture of the stone, as the artist's attention was not focused on them. Monet needed the façade merely as an elaborate flat surface for a masterly recording of every nuance of lighting.

The sun shines from the south, so that the surface of the west façade is partly or completely shadowed, and only some surfaces of the relief details are lit by rays of sunlight.

There are very close paintings showing the west façade of Rouen Cathedral in the Musée d'Orsay in Paris (W., III, 1346, 1355, 1360).

The numerous pale patches of blue, violet and orange-golden hues turn the façade into a kind of coloured lace, all of which, both in the sun and in the shade, is permeated with light and air. This profoundly poetic and highly original image attests to the artist's keen powers of observation and rich imagination.

Monet worked passionately on the series. In March 1893 he wrote to Paul Durand-Ruel: "I am working to the best of my ability, but I cannot even dream of doing anything besides the cathedral. The work is enormous" (W., III, 1304). Wildenstein assigns the picture to 1893, supposing that later Monet dated the whole series to 1894.

Provenance: 1898 P. Durand-Ruel collection, Paris; 1902 S. Shchukin collection, Moscow; 1918 First Museum of Modern Western Painting, Moscow; 1928 Museum of Modern Western Art, Moscow; after 1948 Pushkin Museum of Fine Arts, Moscow.

Exhibitions: 1985 Paris; 1955 Moscow (Cat., p. 47); 1960 Moscow (Cat., p. 29); 1974 Leningrad (Cat. No. 27); 1974-1975 Moscow (Cat. No. 21)

105.

WINTER LANDSCAPE

(Sandviken) 1895.
Oil on cardboard. 37 x 52.5 cm
Signed, bottom right: Claude Monet.
The Latvian Republican Museum
of Foreign Art, Riga.
Inventory No. 517.

L ate in January 1895, Monet travelled to Scandinavia. On February 26 he wrote from Sandviken to his friend Gustave Geffroy: "I have at last found a suitable spot and settled here. I have already spent a few days working and started eight canvases, which I hope, if the weather favours me, will give you an idea of Norway and the environs of Christiania…. This morning I was painting under constantly falling snow. You would have burst out laughing seeing me white all over, my beard overgrown with icicles." (Geffroy 1922, vol. 2, pp. 87, 88).

The *Winter Landscape*, painted during Monet's stay at Sandviken, recorded the severe Norwegian winter, faithfully re-creating the atmosphere of a frosty day. The houses, the trees and the hill are shrouded in a haze which melts their contours, softening and subduing the harmonious colours. The white blanket of snow seems to radiate light, creating a diversity of tints, reflections and subtle transitions of colour. The darker patches of the reddish houses and the brownish little bridge enliven the dominant light colour scheme. The trees are only partly covered with snow.

The painting is notable for its varied handling of texture. The direction of the strokes follows the shapes of the objects: thus the woody hillside is painted with brief vertical dashes, the snow with horizontal dabs and the bridge with curving touches that bring out its bend.

This site appears also in three other paintings (W., III, 1397; W., III, 1398; W., III, 1399).

84. *Sandviken Village under the Snow*,
The Art Institute of Chicago.

Provenance: K. Jurjanis collection, Riga; after 1946 The Latvian Republican Museum of Foreign Art, Riga.

Exhibitions: 1955 Riga.

85. *Kolsaas Mountain, Misty Weather*, 1895.

86. *Kolsaas Mountain*, 1895.

WHITE WATER-LILIES

1899.
Oil on canvas. 89 x 93 cm.
Signed and dated, bottom left:
Claude Monet 99.
The Pushkin Museum of Fine Arts, Moscow.
Inventory No. 3309.

After settling at Giverny in 1883, Monet bought a plot of land there. He had water diverted from the Epte River and laid out a water-garden, with ponds where water-lilies of various shades were grown and changed several times a year. This became the artist's cherished creation, and not surprisingly, the motif of the water-garden at Giverny became an important element in Monet's work, especially from the late 1890s.

Particularly significant among the landscapes produced at Giverny is the series *Water-lilies* (*Les Nymphéas*), which was painted between 1898 and 1908 and comprised forty-eight landscape scenes. The entire series was shown at Durand-Ruel's in 1909. This, however, was not the end of Monet's work on the subject: in 1915 he returned to the water-lilies motif and painted a series of large panels, which would later decorate the walls of the Orangerie and the Musée Marmottan in Paris.

The present painting is one of the earliest (1899) and best-known in the series, as is its close version from the Musée d'Orsay in Paris (1899, R.F. 2004).

The Moscow canvas shows a garden corner with a pond covered with pinkish-white and yellow water-lilies and their large green leaves. A light wooden "Japanese" bridge arches over the pond surrounded with the verdure of the garden, only a little patch of the deep blue sky showing through the foliage. The intense white, pink and yellow dabs of the water-lilies stand out in sharp relief against the prevailing deep green of the background. In this series Monet's prime concern was the harmony of colour. It is no longer the transient state of nature, atmosphere and lighting that fascinates him — much more it is the decorative value of various combinations of colour. Since about 1898, the same problems had interested Marquet and Matisse, the future originators of Fauvism. It is worthy of note that the ageing Monet also kept searching for new motifs and new painting techniques. In the present painting the artist employed a more diversified brushwork, his stokes now assuming the shape of commas, as in the green plants by the water, now impasted dots or unbroken lines distinctly outlining the small bridge rising over the pond.

These devices made the palette in this picture richer and more varied, the pictorial statement more clear-cut and definite — a far cry from the early stage of Impressionism ended long before.

Provenance: S. Shchukin collection; 1918 First Museum of Modern Western Painting, Moscow; 1929 Museum of Modern Western Art, Moscow; after 1948 Pushkin Museum of Fine Arts, Moscow.

Exhibitions: 1909 Paris; 1939 Moscow (Cat., p. 48); 1955 Moscow (Cat., p. 48); 1960 Moscow (Cat., p. 28); 1974-1975 Moscow (Cat. No. 22).

88. *Pond with Water-lilies*, 1897-1899. The Art Museum, Princeton University, Princeton, New Jersey.

89. **Pink Water-lilies**, 1897-1899. Galleria Nazionale d'Arte Moderna, Roma.

VÉTHEUIL

1901.
Oil on canvas. 90 x 92 cm.
Signed and dated, bottom left:
Claude Monet 1901.
The Pushkin Museum of Fine Arts, Moscow.
Inventory No. 3314.

Light-coloured houses with reddish roofs are scattered amidst the verdure covering the hill at the riverside, the tower of the town church rising in the middle. This is the small town of Vétheuil whose buildings are reflected in the water of the river occupying the foreground. The painting is a distant view from the opposite bank of the river, so that the buildings are shown as a solid mass. In this picture there are no distinct linear contours and no contrasting patches of light, as everything is shrouded in thin haze. The coarse-textured brushwork knit from small strokes lend a tapestry-like appearance to the surface of the canvas.

Monet first took up the motif of Vétheuil in 1878, after moving there from Argenteuil, and worked regularly on it henceforth. Most of his views of Vétheuil date from the years 1878-1882.

In 1883 the artist moved to Giverny, but he occasionally paid visits to Vétheuil, working on the familiar subjects there, and some of the most famous pictures of that town were painted during his sojourn of 1901.

The present painting was also created at that time. In the Institute of Art in Chicago there are two other canvases showing Vétheuil and dating from the same year.

Provenance: 1902 Bernheim-Jeune collection, Paris; 1902 P. Durand-Ruel collection, Paris; 1902 S. Shchukin collection, Moscow; 1918 First Museum of Modern Western Painting, Moscow; 1928 Museum of Modern Western Art, Moscow; after 1948 Pushkin Museum of Fine Arts, Moscow.

Exhibitions: 1939 Moscow (Cat., p. 48); 1960 Moscow (Cat., p. 29); 1973 Washington, New York... Detroit (Cat. No. 28); 1974 Leningrad (Cat. No. 29); 1974-1975 Moscow (Cat. No. 23).

91. ***Snow Effects in Vétheuil or Church in Vétheuil, Snow***, 1878-1879. Musée d'Orsay, Paris.

92. ***Monet's Garden in Vétheuil***, 1881. National Gallery of Art, Washington (DC).

93.

ON THE CLIFFS
NEAR DIEPPE

1897.
Oil on canvas. 64.5 x 100 cm.
Signed and dated, bottom right:
Claude Monet. 97.
The Hermitage, St. Petersburg.
Inventory No. 8992. W., III, 1467.

Monet went to the ocean coast of Normandy late in January 1897 hoping to resume work on his sketches of the winter sea begun the previous year. He stayed at Pourville near Dieppe and on April 1 wrote to Paul Durand-Ruel that he was working hard in spite of bad weather. The artist's hard work resulted, in the space of three months, in a group of landscapes — *The Cliffs near Dieppe* (W., III, 1433, 1434, 1465, 1471).

The impression evoked by the picture *On the Cliffs near Dieppe* corresponds rather closely with the description of the scene given by the writer Eugène Fromantin in his novel Dominique in 1862: "One had to strain one's eyes to see where the sea ended and the sky began — so much alike were they in their turbid paleness, their stormy trepidation and their boundlessness, and border line between them obliterated." Monet was the first nineteenth-century landscape painter in France to give expression to this infinity and to the merging of the two elements. The cliffs, sea and

sky are shrouded in a morning dew mist, which blurs all the outlines. The artist's main concern is to render the minutest colour fluctuations in the atmosphere. The picture displays features characteristic of a whole period of Monet's work, for example, a composition not dependent for support on vertical lines and a fluidity of form, here brought out particularly by the austere curve.

This fascination with the subtlest effects of light and air, with scenes suffused with haze, was to bring Monet, two years later, to the banks of the Thames.

In 1898 the present canvas was apparently exhibited, along with a large series of Norman landscapes, at the George Petit Gallery. In 1900 the artist informed Paul Durand-Ruel in his letter of January 23, that he was sending him, among other landscapes, the picture *On the Cliffs near Dieppe*.

There is a drawing from Monet's note-book of the 1880s, which depicts a very similar motif, in the Musée Marmottan in Paris (Inv. No. 5131).

Provenance: 1901 P. Durand-Ruel collection, Paris; 1903 S. Shchukin collection, Moscow; 1918 First Museum of Modern Western Painting, Moscow; 1928 Museum of Modern Western Art, Moscow; after 1948 Hermitage, Leningrad.

Exhibitions: 1974 Leningrad (Cat. No. 28); 1975 Budapest (Cat. No. 19); 1979 Kyoto, Tokyo, Kamakura (Cat. No. 9).

94. *At the Val Saint-Nicolas, near Dieppe, in the Morning*, 1897.

95. *The Tip of the Petit Ailly, Cloudy Weather*, 1897.

WATERLOO BRIDGE

1903.
Formerly entitled Fog in London
(Waterloo Bridge).
Oil on canvas. 65 x 100 cm.
Signed and dated, bottom right:
Claude Monet 1903.
The Hermitage, St. Petersburg.
Inventory No. 6545.

In 1899-1901 Monet went to London for the winters, staying at the Savoy Hotel. The balcony of his room opened on to the Thames, with Waterloo Bridge on the left and factory chimneys smoking behind it.

This view inspired a whole series of paintings showing Waterloo Bridge. After 1901 the artist dispensed with plein-air studies, completing his London landscapes in his studio at Giverny — a practice uncharacteristic of his earlier period. It was perhaps this absence of direct observation that caused the artist some difficulty, for he often complained in his letters to Paul Durand-Ruel that he lacked inspiration. Though the pictures of this group are of uneven artistic quality, the series is quite significant. While working on it Monet became convinced that direct observation was insufficient for recreating the subtle colouristic harmonies produced by fog, which transformed everything into barely discernible ephemeral silhouettes. Therefore, repeating the same motifs, the artist now strove to fashion his luminous visions of colour without immediate contact with the actual location. He was less interested in the architectural beauties of the place than in the infinite variations of atmospheric effects caused by rays of sunshine penetrating the fog.

A series of views of London is the most extensive cycle in Monet's work. It comprises over one hundred works housed now in various museums and private collections scattered all over the world. According to the motif portrayed the series is conventionally divided into three groups: Waterloo Bridge, Charing Cross Bridge and the House of Parliament. The artist must have begun the first group, including the Hermitage painting, in 1900 (judging by the date indicated in the catalogue of the exhibition held in the Durand-Ruel Gallery in 1904, No. 9), and completed it in 1903 at Giverny.

The title is based on the inscription on the back of P. Durand-Ruel's label: *Waterloo Bridge. Effect of Mist*. There is a pastel entitled *Waterloo Bridge* with the same motif in the Musée Marmottan in Paris (Inv. No. 5048).

Provenance: 1906 P. Durand-Ruel collection, Paris; 1907 I. Morozov collection, Moscow; 1918 Second Museum of Modern Western Painting, Moscow; 1928 Museum of Modern Western Art, Moscow; after 1930 Hermitage, Leningrad.

Exhibitions: 1904 Paris (Cat. No. 19 or 20); 1955 Moscow (Cat., p. 48); 1956 Leningrad (Cat., p. 42); 1965 Berlin (Cat. No. 8); 1973 Warsaw (Cat. No. 17); 1974 Leningrad (Cat. No. 30); 1974-1975 Moscow (Cat. No. 24); 1976 Dresden (Cat. No. 8); 1979 Kyoto, Tokyo, Kamakura (Cat. No. 11); 1981 Mexico (Cat. No. 22)

97. *London, Waterloo Bridge*, 1899-1901.

98. *Charing Cross Bridge, Cloudy Weather*, 1899-1901.

126.

99. *Waterloo Bridge, Cloudy Weather*, 1899-1901.

SEAGULLS (THE THAMES IN LONDON. THE HOUSES OF PARLIAMENT)

1904.

Oil on canvas. 82 x 92 cm.

Signed and dated, bottom right:

Claude Monet 1904.

The Pushkin Museum of Fine Arts, Moscow.

Inventory No. 3306.

Monet made his first journey to London in 1870-1871. Later he repeatedly visited the city and stayed there for long periods. In 1899-1904 he painted his famous series of London views. The present canvas is one of the artist's eleven paintings showing the motif of the Houses of Parliament. The picture is dated 1904 and thus belongs to the final works in the series.

Few painters depicting London have been able to render the atmospheric effects typical of the city so convincingly. In 1904 thirty-seven canvases from the London series, including the present painting, were displayed at the Durand-Ruel Gallery in Paris. These views are now to be found in many collections in different parts of the world, notably in Paris, Chicago, Hamburg and New York.

Provenance: 1904 P. Durand-Ruel collection, Paris; 1904 S. Shchukin collection, Moscow; 1918 First Museum of Modern Western Painting, Moscow; 1928 Museum of Modern Western Art, Moscow Art, Moscow; after 1948 Pushkin Museum of Fine Arts, Moscow.

Exhibitions: 1904 Paris; 1939 Moscow (Cat., p 48); 1955 Moscow (Cat., p. 48); 1960 Moscow (Cat., p. 29); 1971 Tokyo. Kyoto (Cat. No. 50); 1974 Leningrad (Cat. No. 31); 1974-1975 Moscow (Cat. No. 25).

101. *The Thames River and the Houses of Parliament*, 1871.

102. ***The Houses of Parliament, Sunset***, 1900-1901. The Brooklyn Museum, New York.

103. **London, *The Houses of Parliament*, *Effects of Sunlight in Fog***, 1904. Oil on canvas, 81x92 cm. Musée d'Orsay, Paris.

104. *The Grand Canal*, 1908. Museum of Fine Arts, Boston, Massachussetts

105. *The Doge's Palace*, 1908. Mr and Mrs Herbert J. Klapper.

106. *The Dario Palace*, 1908. The Art Institute of Chicago.

107. *Impression*: *Sunrise*, 1873. Musée Marmottan, Paris.

108. *Mill in Zaandaam*, 1871.

$\mathcal{M}$onet 1840-1926 : Chronology

1840

November 14: Claude Oscar Monet is born in Paris.

1845

The Monet family moves to Le Havre.

1858

Makes the acquaintance of Boudin, who introduces him to plein-air painting.

1859

Goes to Paris. Meets Troyon. Frequents the Académie Suisse, where he meets Pissarro.

1860

Draws at the Académie Suisse. Paints landscapes at Champigny-sur-Marne. In the autumn, is called up for military service.

1861

Serves with the army in Algeria.

1862

Discharged for health reasons. In the summer, works at Sainte-Adresse together with Boudin and Jongkind. In November, returns to Paris. Attends the studio of Gleyre. Meets Renoir, Sisley and Bazille.

1863

Works at Chailly-en-Bière near Fontainebleau. At the end of the year Monet, Renoir, Sisley and Bazille leave the studio of Gleyre.

1864

Works at Honfleur with Bazille, Boudin and Jongkind. In Paris, meets Gustave Courbet.

1865

Exhibits two seascapes in the Salon. Spends the summer at Chailly together with Bazille. In the autumn, works at Trouville with Courbet, Daubigny and Whistler.

1866

Paints views of Paris. Exhibits *Woman in a Green Dress* (Camille) in the Salon. Meets Edouard Manet. At Ville d'Avray, paints *Women in the Garden*; in Le Havre, *The Jetty at Le Havre*; then works at Sainte-Adresse and Honfleur.

1867

Experiences financial hardship. Lives with his parents at Sainte-Adresse. In the autumn, returns to Paris.

1868

Works at Étretat and Fécamp.

1869

Together with Renoir, works at Bougival, where he paints *La Grenouillère*. Moves to Étretat, then to Le Havre.

1870

In September, goes to London.

1871

Stays in London. Daubigny introduces him to Durand-Ruel. Meets Pissarro. Travels to Holland. Reveals an interest in Japanese prints. Returns to France visiting Belgium on his way. In December, stays at Argenteuil.

1872

Together with Boudin, visits Courbet imprisoned for his participation in the Commune. Works at Le Havre, where he paints *Impression: Sunrise*. After his second trip to Holland settles at Argenteuil (until 1878).

1873

Works at Argenteuil in a studio boat, painting the banks of the Seine.

1874

Shows nine works at the exhibition later to be called the First Impressionist Exhibition held at Nadar's (April 15 – May 15, 35 Boulevard des Capucines). Meets Caillebotte.

1875

Continues to work at Argenteuil. Difficult financial situation.

1876

In April, takes part in the Second Impressionist Exhibition, at the Durand-Ruel Gallery (11 Rue Le Peletier), showing eighteen works. Begins the Gare Saint-Lazare series, which he finishes the next year.

1877

In April, participates in the Third Impressionist Exhibition (6 Rue Le Peletier), displaying thirty paintings. Visits Montgeron. In the winter, returns to Paris.

1878

Settles at Vétheuil.

1879

At the Fourth Impressionist Exhibition (April 10-May 11, 28 Avenue de l'Opera) shows twenty-nine paintings. Works at Vétheuil and Lavacourt.

1880

His one-man show at the premises of the newspaper *La Vie Moderne*. Works at Vétheuil.

1881

Works at Vétheuil, Fécamp and, in December, at Poissy.

1882

In March, at the Seventh Impressionist Exhibition (251 Rue Saint-Honoré) shows thirty-five paintings. Works at Pourville, Dieppe and Poissy.

109. *Monet*, Summer 1926.
Photograph Nickolas Murray.
The Museum of Modern Art, New York.

110. *Claude Monet on the Japanese Bridge*, 1925,
Archives Clemenceau Museum, Paris.

1883

In March, his one-man show at the Durand-Ruel Gallery. In May, stays at Giverny. Works in the environs of Vernon, in Le Havre, and at Étretat. In December, makes a short trip to the Mediterranean with Renoir. Visits Cézanne at l'Estaque.

1884

From January 17 to March 14, works at Bordighera. In April, stays at Menton; in August, at Étretat; in the autumn, at Giverny.

1885

Takes part in the International Exhibition at the Georges Petit Gallery. From October to December, works at Étretat.

1886

A brief trip to Holland. Refuses to take part in the Eighth (last) Impressionist Exhibition. Contributes to the International Exhibition at the Georges Petit Gallery. A show of Monet's paintings in New York. In September, works at Belle-Île, where he meets Geoffroy.

1887

Shows two paintings at the Exhibition of the Royal Society of British Artists in London.

1888

From January to April, lives at Antibes. In July, visits London. In September, return to Étretat.

1889

In July, exhibition of works by Monet and Rodin (145 pieces) in the Georges Petit Gallery.

1890

Begins the Haystacks and Poplars series. Moves to Giverny.

1891

Continues his work on the Haystacks and Poplars series. The Haystacks series enjoys a success at the exhibition in the Durand-Ruel Gallery. In December, visits London.

1892

Exhibits his Poplars series. Begins the Rouen Cathedral series.

1893

Continues his work on the Rouen Cathedral series.

1894

Cézanne visits Giverny.

1895

In January, travels to Norway. Shows his Cathedrals series in the Durand-Ruel Gallery (May 10-31).

1896

In February and March, works at Pourville.

1897

From January to March, stays at Pourville.

1898

In June, takes part in the exhibition at the Georges Petit Gallery.

1899

Begins the Water-Lilies. In the autumn, goes to London, where he paints views of the Thames.

1900

In February, visits London again. In April, works at Giverny. Spends the summer at Vétheuil.

1901

In February and April, stays in London.

1902

Spends February and March in Brittany.

1903

Works on views of the Thames in London.

1904

Paints his garden at Giverny. Shows his views of the Thames at the exhibition in the Durand-Ruel Gallery (May 9-June 14). In October, goes to Madrid to see works by Velázquez.

1906

Works on the Water-Lilies series.

1908

From September to December, stays in Venice.

1909

In the autumn, returns to Venice, where he paints a series of views.

1912

Shows his Venetian series at the exhibition in the Bernhein-Jeune Gallery (May 28-June 8).

1916

Begins work on the decorative panels the Water-lilies.

1921

A retrospective exhibition in the Durand-Ruel Gallery
(January 21-February 2). In September, a short trip to Brittany.

1922

Suffers from eye disease.

1923

Works on the decorative panels the Water-Lilies.

1926

December 5 dies at Giverny.

111. *The Wooden Bridge*, 1872. Fondation Rau pour le Tiers-Monde, Zurich.

112. *Three Fishing Boats*, 1885. Budapest.

Exhibitions

1874, Paris
Société anonyme des artistes, peintres, sculpteurs, graveurs, etc. 35,
Boulevard des Capucines. Première exposition. Paris, 1874.

1877, Paris
Troisième Exposition de peinture (April). Paris, 1877.

1879, Paris
Quatrième Exposition de peinture. Paris, 1879.

1889, Paris
Georges Petit Gallery. Claude Monet et Auguste Rodin. Paris, 1889.

1895, Paris
Durand-Ruel Gallery. Claude Monet. Vues de la Cathédrale de Rouen.
Paris, 1895.

1900, Paris
Grand Palais. Exposition Universelle. Paris 1900.

1903, Vienna
Vereinigung Bildender Künstler. Österreich Secession. XVI.
Vienna, 1903.

1904, Paris
9 mai-4 juin. Durand-Ruel Gallery. Claude Monet: Vues de la Tamise à
Londres (1902-1904). Paris, 1904.

1906, Paris
Durand-Ruel Gallery. Dix-sept tableaux de Claude Monet de la collection
J.-B. Faure. Paris, 1906.

1906, Berlin, Stuttgart
Paul Cassirer Gallery. Manet-Monet. Sammlung J.-B. Faure. Berlin, 1906.

1907, Mannheim
1st May-20th October. Städtische Kunsthalle. Internationale
Kunstausstellung. Mannheim, 1907.

1909, Paris
Durand-Ruel Gallery. Claude-Monet. Paris, 1909.

1939, Moscow
Museum of Modern Western Art. French Landscape Painting. Nineteenth
and Twentieth Centuries. Moscow, 1939 (Catalogue in Russian).

1955, Moscow
The Pushkin Museum of Fine Arts. Exhibition of French Art: Fifteenth to Twentieth Century. Moscow, 1955 (Catalogue in Russian).

1955, Riga
Art Museum of the Latvian SSR. Western European Art: Early Twentieth Century. Riga, 1955 (Catalogue in Latvian).

1956, Leningrad
The Hermitage. French Art: Twelfth to Twentieth Centuries. Leningrad, 1956 (Catalogue in Russian).

1960, Moscow
The Pushkin Museum of Fine Arts. Exhibition of French Art of the Second Half of the Nineteenth Century from the Reserves of Soviet Art Museums. Moscow, 1960 (Catalogue in Russian).

1965, Berlin
National Galerie. Von Delacroix bis Picasso, Berlin, 1965.

1965-1966, Bordeaux, Paris
14 mai-6 septembre. Museum of Fine Arts. September 1965-January 1966. Musée du Louvre. Chefs-d'œuvre de la peinture française dans les musées de Leningrad et de Moscou. Paris, 1965.

1966-1967, Tokyo, Kyoto
Masterpieces of Modern Painting from the USSR. Tokyo, 1966.

1971, Tokyo, Kyoto
Tokyo. April 10-May 30. Kyoto June 8-July 25. One hundred Masterpieces from the USSR. Tokyo, 1971.

1972, Otterlo
April 30-July 16. State Museum Kröller-Müller. From Van Gogh to Picasso. Exhibition from the Pushkin Museum in Moscow and the Hermitage in Leningrad. Otterlo, 1972.

1972, Prague
Národní Galerie. Kresby evropskych mistru XV-XX století ze sbírek státní Ermitáze v Leningrade. Prague, 1972.
1973, Washington, New York,... Chicago...
Washington. National Gallery of Art. New York. M. Knoedler and Co. Los Angeles. County Museum of Arts. Chicago. The Art Institute. Port-Worth. The Kimbel Art Museum. Detroit. The Institute of Arts. Impressionists and Postimpressionists Painting from the USSR. New York, 1973.

1973, Warsaw
Warszawa. Museum Narodowe. Malarstwo francuskie XVII-XX wieków ze zbiórow Ermitazu. Warsaw, 1973.

113. *The Havre Harbour during the Night*, 1873. Private collection.

1974, Leningrad
The Hermitage. Impressionist Painting. The Centenary of the
First Impressionist Exhibition of 1874. Leningrad. 1974
(Catalogue in Russian).

1974-1975, Moscow
The Pushkin Museum of Fine Arts. Impressionist Painting. The
Centenary of the First Exhibition of the Impressionists: 1874-1974.
Moscow, 1974 (Catalogue in Russian).
1974-1975, Paris, New York
L'Impressionnisme. Exposition du centenaire. Paris-New York, 1974.

1975, Budapest
Szépmuvészeti museum Remekmuvek a Szovjetunio muzeumaibol.
A kiallitas az alabbi gyujtemények anyagabol készult valogas.
Ermitazs Allami Tretiakov keptar. Budapest, 1975.

1975, Moscow
The Pushkin Museum of Fine Arts. Fifty Years of Diplomatic
Relations between France and the USSR. Moscow, 1975
(Catalogue in Russian).

1976, Dresden
18 September-31 October. Albertinum. Meisterwerke aus dem
Puschkin-Museum, Moskau und der Ermitage, Leningrad.
Dresden, 1976.

1978, Le havre
23 May-3 July. Musée des Beaux-Arts André Malraux. La peinture
impressionniste et postimpressionniste du Musée de l'Ermitage.
Le Havre, 1978.

1979, Kyoto, Tokyo, Kamakura
French painters, late 19th century-early 20 th century from the
Hermitage and The Pushkin Museum of fine arts. Tokyo, 1979.

1980, Paris
5 February-5 May. Grand Palais. Hommage à Claude Monet
(1840-1926). Paris, 1980.

1981, Mexico
Museo del Palacio de Bellas Artes (Sala Nacional Cultural).
Impresionistas franceses de los museos Ermitage y Pushkin.
Mexico, 1981.

114. *The Painter with a Pointed Hat*, drawing.

115. *Boat Being Repaired*, 1881. Tokyo Fuji Art Museum.

116. *Man with a Straw Hat*, ca. 1857. Musée Marmottan, Paris.

BARSKAYA

A. Barskaya, Claude Monet, Leningrad, 1980.

BARSKAYA, IZERGINA

A. Barskaya, A. Izergina, French Painting. Second Half of the 19th to Early 20th Century. Hermitage Museum, Leningrad, 1975.

CATALOGUE. MOSCOW

Catalogue of Paintings in the S. Shchukin Collection, Moscow, 1913.

CATALOGUE. MOSCOW

Catalogue of the Museum of Modern Western Art, Moscow, 1928.

CATALOGUE. MOSCOW

Catalogue of the Picture Gallery of the Pushkin Museum of Fine Arts, Moscow, 1957.

CATALOGUE 1958

Catalogue of Paintings. Hermitage Museum. Department of Western European Art, Leningrad-Moscow, 1958, vol. 1.

CATALOGUE. MOSCOW

Catalogue of the Picture Gallery of the Pushkin Museum of Fine Arts. Moscow, 1961.

CATALOGUE 1976

Catalogue of Paintings. Hermitage Museum. Department of Western European Art, vol. 1, Leningrad, 1976.

GEFFROY

G. Geffroy, Claude Monet. Sa vie, son temps, son œuvre, vols. 1, 2, paris, 1922.

GEORGIEVSKAYA

E. Georgievskaya, Claude Monet, Moscow, 1973.

GEORGIEVSKAYA, KUZNETSOVA

E. Georgievskaya, I. Kuznetsova, French Painting from the Pushkin Museum of Fine Art, Leningrad, 1980.

MAKOVSKY

S. Makovsky, French Artistsin the I. A. Morozov, Collection, "Apollon", No 3-4, 1912.

MONET. ALBUM

Claude Monet. Album, Leningrad, 1969.

ORLOVA

M. Orlova, Claude Monet, "Iskusstvo", 1940, No 6.

PATAKY

    D. Pataky, Monet, Budapest, 1966.

PERTSOV

    P. Pertsov, The Shchukin Collection of French Painting,
    Moscow, 1921.

PROKOFIEV

    V. Prokoviev, French Paintings in the Museums
    of the U.S.S.R., 1962.

RÉAU

    L. Réau, Catalogue de l'art français dans les musées russes,
    Paris, 1929.

REUTERSWÄRD 1948

    O. Reuterswärd, Claude Monet, Stockholm, 1948.

REUTERSWÄRD 1965

    O. Reuterswärd, Claude Monet, Stockholm, 1948; Abridged Russian translation: Moscow 1965.

REWALD 1959

    J. Rewald, The History of Impressionism, New York, 1946; Russian translation: Leningrad-Moscow, 1959.

REWALD 1961

    J. Rewald, The History of Impressionism, New York, 1961.

STERLING

    Ch. Sterling, Musée de l'Ermitage. La Peinture française de Poussin à nos jours, Paris, 1957.

TERNOVETS

    B. Ternovets, Musée d'Art Moderne de Moscou, "L'Amour de l'Art", décembre 1925.

TUGENDHOLD 1914

    Y. Tugendhold, The Shchukin Collection of French Painting, "Apollo", 1914, No 1-2.

TUGENDHOLD 1923

    Y. Tugendhold, The First Museum of Modern Western Painting. The S. Shchukin Collection, Moscow-Petrograd, 1923.

VENTURI

    L. Venturi, Les Archives de l'Impressionnisme, Paris-New York, 1939, vols. 1, 2.

WERTH

    L. Werth, Claude Monet, Paris, 1928.

WILDENSTEIN (OR w.)

    D. Wildenstein, Claude Monet. Biographie et catalogue raisonné, vol. 1, Lausanne-Paris, 1974; vols. 2, 3, Lausanne-Paris, 1979.

117. *Black Woman with Madras*, c. 1857. Musée Marmottan, Paris.

118. *The Varangeville Church, Morning Effect*, 1882.

119. *The Cliff at Étretat, after the Storm*, 1870. Musée d'Orsay, Paris.

120. *Monet in his Garden*, Summer 1905. Photograph by Bulloz.

Index

121. *The Pond with Water-Lilies*, 1917-1919.

Claude Monet